*What makes you feel
you must suffer in silence?*

TURN YOUR PAIN INTO POWER

Suffering in Silence

JOANNE R. KANUTE

Presented by Unlimited Creations in conjunction with
Heritage Press Publications, LLC
PO Box 561
Collinsville, MS 39325

ISBN: 9781945464317
eBook ISBN: 9781945464324

Cover Design: Christine E. Dupre
Interior Design: Lisa Thomson

Dedication

This book was greatly inspired, influenced, and is dedicated to my mother, Betty. After our dad passed in 2002, our mother moved onto our property. She had her own little two-bedroom, two-bath manufactured home on our property in Tucson, Arizona, and she was so proud of it! She would tell everyone, "This is the very first home I have ever owned all by myself." Yes, it was very cute and just right for her! During the six and a half years she lived by us, I was able to learn so much more about my mother.

As it became more challenging for her to be able to live alone in her little home due to the beginning stages of Alzheimer's and numerous other health issues, she decided she wanted to move back to North Dakota as she still called it "home." Sad to say, she passed away only a few short weeks upon her return to North Dakota. We were sad to see her move, but we wanted her to be able to fulfil her wish—and she did!

While she lived in Tucson, she would pass some of the time by coming to work with me three days a week. We owned a hair salon and she would wash and fold towels, make coffee, and serve cookies. We also had a boutique in our salon and she loved to move things around and show the clients some of the new merchandise. As her dementia/Alzheimer's progressed, she lost interest in coming to the salon or doing any of the things she used to enjoy.

She felt like she was becoming a burden to me and our family. There were more and more things she wasn't able to do for herself. She was on so many prescription medications that I would fill her pill boxes for two weeks at a time with the help of a spreadsheet.

We always had her join us for dinner because I wanted to make sure she had at least one good meal a day. She reached a point that she wouldn't come over to eat; she felt like she was being too much trouble for us. I would take a meal over to her in her little home and tell her we had leftovers so she should eat them! If she thought they were leftovers and thought I might throw them out, she would eat. Alzheimer's is a disease in which you soon realize you must play many games with its victims so they can continue with life.

After a few weeks of spending time in the salon, my mother said, "When you get those clients back to the shampoo bowl and they lean back, it is like their jaws come unhinged." She was referring to the conversations and stories she heard in passing throughout the salon. Many times, she was amazed at what clients would tell us.

One day she came to me and said, "Please tell your clients NO ONE should ever suffer in silence like I have most of my life. Tell all the

women you come in contact with to NEVER suffer in silence." That is a statement I will never forget for the rest of my life! It also is a statement I will do my best to fulfill because it was my mother's wishes. It is this statement that has challenged me to pursue my education in order to be equipped with the tools needed to fulfill her wishes—helping women to find their purpose and to keep moving forward even when it hurts!

Table of Contents

Chapter 1   **Pain Into Power** 5
- Loneliness 7
- Bitterness 11
- Forgiveness 14

Chapter 2   **Communication is Key** 21
- Where's Your Voice 25
- Conflict and Confrontation 31
- Assertive 35

Chapter 3   **Forms of Abuse** 41
- Emotional 43
- Psychological 43
- Narcissist – Manipulator – Gaslighter 54

Chapter 4   **Cheater Cheater** 95
- Trust and Lies 95
- Relationships 100
- Fear 115

Chapter 5   **Emotional Rollercoaster** 119
- Rageaholic – Anger 119
- Stress and Anxiety 127
- Setting Healthy Boundaries 136

Chapter 6   **Dealing with Rejection** 145

  • ABCs of Rejection 146

  • Painful 149

  • Root of Rejection 150

Chapter 7   **Money Does Matter** 153

  • Spend – Save 155

  • Financial Abuse 158

  • Future – Retirement 164

Chapter 8   **Moving Forward** 169

  • Believe In Yourself 169

  • Clear The Clutter 177

  • Goal Setting 183

Chapter 9   **Build Your Team** 191

  • Same Destination 191

  • Common Traits 196

  • Support and Trust 198

Chapter 10   **Power of a Positive Self-Image** 201

  • What is a Self-Image and Self-Esteem 201

  • Self-Care 214

  • Self-Worth and Attitude 220

Chapter 11   **What's Your Story** 229

  • Past 229

  • Present 233

  • Future 235

Preface

On a daily basis we will find that life can truly be challenging. As we walk the path of life, we often times will hit a number of speed bumps in our travels. There are many hills to climb, many curves that come our way we can't see around, as well as the deep ditches along the road that we sometimes find ourselves stuck in! I believe God has a purpose and a plan for each and every one of our lives. Yes, life can bring much pain, but...

What we need to do is turn that experience of pain into power!

I want to inspire others to leave their past behind so that they can explore, grow, and move forward with their lives! We all can find reasons to get stuck in self-pity, but we don't allow ourselves to stay there. During my childhood I was told several times a week I was fat, ugly, dumb, and would never amount to a thing! This was a battle I carried into my earlier adult years. Did it ever completely disappear? No, these battles don't, but we must gain control over them in order to move forward with our journey in life.

In my later years of life, I came to learn my earthly father was what we now know as a narcissist with verbal abuse tendencies. He thought about himself first and he was concerned with what other people might think about him. He had an image to project to the world, but what went on within the walls of our big old simple farmhouse didn't always match. Growing up on a farm in the very rural area of North Dakota, there was always work that needed to be done. Once again, on a weekly basis we heard, "I had you kids (yep, there were six of us) to help with the farm, now get busy."

The word "narcissist" is a word that is becoming all too familiar in today's society. What is a narcissist, you may ask? A narcissist is someone with a personality disorder, a need for admiration, and a lack of empathy. As you read through the book, you will notice this disorder can have many different masks and angles to it. It is quite complex and, depending on the severity, can be a huge hurdle to climb over and deal with.

I'm often asked, "How did you ever overcome those deep wounds?" My answer to you is I have the scars, but the wounds have healed by the help of God! First, I had to forgive. Forgiving doesn't mean you forget. We forgive because it is biblical, and we must forgive so we can move forward. We lived through our past experiences once—why would we want to continue to put ourselves through those experiences over and over? Forgive and move forward with your journey of life. We can learn from our past and use it to make our future stronger due to the past pain. In their 1984 article in *The Ladies Home Journal*, authors Barnett, Baruch, and Rivers stated: "Feeling good about ourselves may, in fact, be the cornerstone of our total well-being."

The Bible says that when we have negative thoughts about ourselves, we are disapproving of the Creator himself. We are created by God, in His image. As Psalm 139:13 says, He knew exactly what he was doing when he knit us together in our mother's womb.

Offering encouraging words to people is so important to me. It helps them look up and ahead instead of looking back and down. I believe God has a purpose and a plan for each and every one of our lives. I am fully committed to encouraging people by walking beside them through the trials of life. I want to inspire others to leave their past behind and to explore, grow, and move forward with their future in Christ. The difference I want to see in the world is people living their full potential for God! At the end of the day, there is no greater feeling than knowing I made a difference in the world by doing what God has called me to do!

Introduction

Allow me to give you a little back story about my mother. She was a very quiet lady and a VERY hard-working woman. Her mother passed away when she was almost three years old. Along with her two brothers, she spent a lot of time with her grandma. Her two brothers, being older than she was, helped their dad on the farm, so they spent a lot of time on the farm and working the land. A couple of years after her mother passed away, her father remarried, and together they had three more children, making a total of six children.

My mom always felt like she didn't totally belong and struggled with self-esteem issues. She hated going to the little country schoolhouse about a mile from their little farmhouse. Let's face it—she didn't like school! Though she didn't like school, she was a very bright woman. At the age of sixteen, she quit school and married our father.

It just seemed like the right thing to do at the time.

More than the right thing to do, she felt it was a way out of the life she wasn't really fitting into.

After a little over a year into their marriage, along came their first son whom they named Marvin. Marvin was born with a heart defect and went through a number of hospital stays and surgery. The doctors were able to bring him back to good health after a last very lengthy hospital stay. The hospital was about four hours away and this was a very difficult experience for our mom. She was away from home, her husband, and any support system. The doctors said once Marvin recovered, he would be able to live a normal healthy life.

When Marvin was nearly two years old, he was involved in a horrible farming accident. He was riding in a grain truck with our mother out to the field. On their way to the field, he leaned against the passenger's side door and the door flung open. Marvin fell out! When our mom got the truck stopped and jumped out to see how he was doing, he was laying lifeless on the ground. It appeared that when he landed on the ground, his head hit a rock.

Mom rushed to our dad in the field to get help and they rushed Marvin to the small nearby hospital that was eighteen miles away. Unfortunately, the doctor was not able to save their little boy.

You can imagine the talk of a little country town and all the different versions of the story being told. As our mom mourned the loss of their son, their first-born child, it was very difficult for her to move forward. But also, as a mother grieving the loss of her child, she found herself crying a lot, and for this she would be told, "Stop your crying!" Our dad did not want her to cry or be sad around the house. He could never say the word depressed or want to hear the word depressed. As far as he was concerned, he needed to get busy and forget about it. Eight months after Marvin's death started the string of six more children within eight years. She was a very busy lady in more ways than one.

Besides caring for six children, our mother did a lot of the farm work and often was found in the field with several kids riding the tractor with her. She was a very hard-working woman and received very little to no appreciation for her hard work. In fact, the next day she was pushed to try to accomplish more!

I truly believe our mother was never really allowed to grieve the loss of their first child and that became a huge struggle for her throughout the rest of her life. Not only did she live with a man that was not pleasant a lot of the time, but she also had a mother-in-law who was openly not fond of her. Our mother didn't seem to measure up to our grandmother's expectations for her first-born son. I will have to say this probably was not a huge surprise, and I'm sure other families have dealt with similar issues.

Why am I telling you the background of my mother's life? This book has eleven chapters discussing many of the issues my mother dealt with, the issues many of you deal with today! My mother named this book even though she is not here for me to tell her that. I know her message to you would be loud and strong: "Don't suffer in silence. Forgive and move forward. You are not hurting anyone but yourself!"

All the issues addressed in this book my mother experienced. This book is not meant to be a "man basher" but examples of true experiences many women have gone through, including my mother. However, many men can also relate to similar or same experiences at a little different level.

Working in the salon industry for over forty years, I mainly work with and on women. The conversations I have and deal with as a life coach behind the salon chair is primarily with women, which is why my book primarily deals with the issues I often hear.

1

Turn Your Pain into Power

"Out of suffering have emerged the strongest souls; the most massive characters are seared with scars." ~ Kahlil Gibran

"To live is to suffer, to survive is to find some meaning in the suffering." ~ Friedrich Nietzsche

Did you know that pain and pleasure sit side by side in your brain? Did you know that repressing your feelings suppresses your immune system?

One of the best secrets on this planet is that all our painful experiences and emotions help us, if we let them. In fact, they are absolutely necessary for our personal growth and our happiness! Just as a battery can't function without both a negative and a positive charge, our "negative emotions" are as essential to our functioning and health as our "positive emotions."

There are two types of pain: One pain hurts you and the other pain changes you. We create our own prisons by judging our experiences and ourselves. Our judgements and our expectations pave the roads to our pain.

Silence doesn't always mean you have nothing to say. It may mean you realize that no matter what you say, it won't change anything and often makes things worse. As people often say, "Pick your battles wisely." People who do not understand your silence will never understand your words. There is a time for silence and then there is a time to find your voice. The greatest accomplishment is to know which is most appropriate for each situation.

Sometimes suffering is just suffering. It doesn't make you stronger. It doesn't build character. It only hurts. Once the heart gets too heavy with pain, people don't even cry. They just turn silent. Completely silent. No response is a response. And it's a powerful one. Never assume that loud is strong and quiet is weak. It's the lion's silence that signals danger, not its roar.

You can never break a woman who finds beauty in everything, even in pain. She turns her scars into wisdom, her struggles into strength, and her setbacks into a comeback. No one was promised life would be easy!

3 Things I know:

1. Prayer does work
2. Tables do turn
3. God is good all the time

Turn Your Problems and Pain into Progress:

- You overthink because you don't write—journal.
- You are anxious because you don't act; you only rehash things in your mind.
- You procrastinate because you don't have a plan—goals are important for progress.

- You stress because you don't train—learn to handle your stress and recognize what your stressors are.
- You lack clarity because you don't journal—when you journal, it helps you see things differently.
- All your problems have a solution; some problems require brainstorming with others.
- You just need to take action—information without action becomes nothing.

What difficult truth are you avoiding or ignoring?

Are you stuck focusing on the negative or are you looking for the positive and to use the experience for good?

Loneliness

"Loneliness is and always has been the central and inevitable experience of every man." ~ Thomas Wolfe

People think that being alone makes you lonely, but I don't think that is true. Being surrounded by the wrong people can be the loneliest place in the world. Feeling alone is a physical state of being by oneself, while loneliness is an emotional state characterized by a sense of isolation and a desire for social connection.

Loneliness is an unpleasant feeling of isolation that can affect people of all ages. We often think loneliness is something only people who live alone experience, but that is not true. You can be around or with people and still experience loneliness. People can experience the feeling of loneliness if a spouse passes away, after a divorce, in bad relationships, after the kids are gone, when the kids are too busy, when our spouse is too busy, when our spouse is distracted or occupied with other things, and on and on.

One thing we need to learn is the difference between feeling alone and feeling lonely—and how you can feel lonely in a crowd full of people but quite peaceful and content when alone. Have you ever heard someone say, "I enjoy my own company"?

If you have experienced abuse, nothing feels more isolating and lonely than watching an abuser receive support from people who should have believed your story but instead embraced the person who broke you. Sometimes God will isolate you before He elevates you. You may think that everything is falling apart, but in reality, everything is falling into place. Just don't allow your loneliness to make you connect with toxic people. You shouldn't drink poison just because you are thirsty.

If you plan to survive loneliness, you need to stay active socially and physically. Even though some of you may be retired, you should continue to set goals for yourself every day. Without goals it is far too easy to pass things off until tomorrow. Push yourself to progress. Make your goals specific, realistic, and important to you. Years ago one of my clients told me she got up every morning and got dressed, and then did her makeup and hair as though she had some place to go. If she didn't need to go any place that day, she would get in her car and just drive around the block. She said it was something she did every single day because it made her feel better!

Get in shape. Exercise helps us to deal with many of the psychological forces that prevent us from making friends. As we move, our bodies release chemicals that help us feel happier and less anxious. As we see improvements in our physical appearance, our self-esteem improves. When we connect with our people, we are less likely to engage in negative behaviors. Getting in shape is something you have complete control over; you are the master of your body.

Here are a few physical goals:

1. **Identify your starting point**—think about your typical weekday and weekend day. Pick activities that are comfortable and enjoyable to you.
2. **Figure out your fitness level**—keep track of how much you exercise or how much you are physically active.
3. **Set short-term goals**—this will help you make physical activity a regular part of your daily life.
4. **Long-term goals**—once you establish your short-term goals, focus on where you want to be in a year, two years, three years, and so on.
5. **Write an exercise plan**—write the "what, when, where, and how much" to your physical exercise plan. Be specific and realistic.

Remaining socially active is very important to your physical and mental health. You may have to stretch out of your comfort zone to meet new friends and find things of interest. It is far too easy to stay home in your comfy clothes and lounge, which often leads to depression! Many ask, "How and where can I meet new people and make new friends?" Here are a few suggestions: volunteer, take a class, join a club (dance, cards, book, stained glass, genealogy, etc.), get involved in your church, connect with your alumni association, senior centers, join a gym, and so on. The possibilities are limitless!

You need to be a friend to have a friend. Be a person others want to be around. A positive upbeat person is more fun to be with than one who is continually negative and complains about things. One of my staff members used to say negative nellies and complainers are "like taking a wet sandwich to a banquet!"

Have you ever been around someone who just sucks the life right of you? Sitting back and waiting for something to change or improve is not going to happen without some effort on your part. There is always a chance of rejection when you reach out to someone. Accept it and don't take it personally. Take responsibility for your life; don't wait for someone else to fix it for you! If you are unhappy with the way your life is going, only **YOU** can change it!

What most people don't realize is that loneliness is a complex problem. Many of us fear rejection; others suffer from low self-esteem or anxiety. Loneliness is continued by a negative twist of actions and emotions, which can very easily become a cycle hard to break. When we are feeling socially isolated, some of us turn to comfort foods or alcohol to dull the pain. If you need alcohol or drugs to love your life, let that be a sign you need to change your life!

Feelings of loneliness and a lack of control go hand in hand. When we take control of the small things in our lives, we start to build a foundation for bigger improvements down the road. It takes time for new patterns to take root, so work on one aspect of your daily routine at a time. You can't rebuild it overnight!

When we are feeling lonely, it is tempting to think that all our problems and negative emotions stem from the fact that we don't have enough friends. This is seldom the case. Most of the time, we are dealing with a range of emotions of which loneliness is just the most obvious.

The problem is we get stuck in our own negative thought patterns and behaviors. Write down one thing you are grateful for every day. Pray for wisdom to see the strength and beauty in you. The healing agents for loneliness are awareness, acceptance, and compassion.

> **Awareness**—pay attention to how your body feels
> **Acceptance**—many people instinctively try to run from loneliness
> **Compassion**—remind yourself others are lonely, too. You are not the only one.

If you're concerned about not having enough friends in your life right now, it's not about numbers, it's about building good relationships. Learn to be your own best friend first!

What thoughts and beliefs contribute to your feelings of loneliness?

"So do not fear, for I am with you; do not be dismayed, for I am your God. I will strengthen you and help you; I will uphold you with my righteous right hand." ~ Isaiah 41:10 (NIV)

Bitterness

Bitterness and resentment only hurt one person, and it's not the person we're resenting—it's us. ~ Alana Stewart

All bitterness starts out as hurt! The ultimate remedy for bitterness is forgiveness. Letting go of grudges and bitterness can make way for happiness, health, and peace. Cry until you laugh if you need to! Laughter is good for your soul and great medicine.

I know from personal experience how damaging it can be to live with bitterness and forgiveness. I like to say it's like taking poison and hoping your enemy will die. And it really is that harmful to us to live this way. ~ Joyce Meyer

In relationships there are many times we are treated unfairly. Resentment is left to fester into bitterness. As women, bitterness is something that many of us struggle with but have a hard time recognizing within ourselves and in our lives.

7 Signs you might struggle with bitterness:

1. You have imaginary conversations
2. You replay a conversation or experience over and over in your head
3. You feel the need to tell someone what he/she did
4. You are easily offended by this person
5. You have strong negative emotional reactions to things they say and do around you
6. You can remember details of things he/she said from months or years ago
7. You are keeping a list of offenses

Many of us are holding onto bitterness as a way to "do something" about what was done to us. We want justice or vengeance for what was done to us and we want it on our terms. I get it. We want to hurt them for what they did to us because it seems like they are getting away with it if we let the wrong go. But by responding this way to a hurt done to you, does it help you or just keep you entrapped in feelings of anger, resentment, and hurt? Being entrapped in bitterness is a vicious cycle that is hard to let go of.

Many people ruin their health and their lives by holding onto the poison of bitterness, resentment, and unforgiveness. It's torture to have hateful thoughts toward another person rolling around inside your head and heart. So many of us are tormented by reliving and rehearsing the past we tightly hold onto, holding grudges, and not letting go. You thought you were just remembering but you are really torturing yourself. My mother held onto bitterness regarding the way she was treated by our grandmother, her mother-in-law, until the last years of her life. She then realized the bitterness was more detrimental to herself than anyone else, but unfortunately allowed herself to suffer for many years.

Steps to break the bitterness cycle:

- The first step toward breaking this cycle is to recognize you are bitter.
- The next step after you recognize you are struggling with bitterness is to begin interrupting your thoughts.
- After you have recognized you are bitter, start listening to what the bitterness is telling you, then take action to correct.

What types of bitterness are/have you dealt with?

Get rid of bitterness, rage and anger, brawling and slander, along with every form of malice. ~ Ephesians 4:31 (NIV)

Forgiveness

Forgiveness is the key to action and freedom. ~ Hannah Arendt

When we forgive people that doesn't mean we accept their behavior or trust them. We forgive them for ourselves so we can let go and move on with our lives.

DO NOT make the mistake of being so understanding and forgiving that you overlook the fact that you're being disrespected. Never tolerate disrespect. Address it in a tactful but firm manner. It is true—when you forgive, you heal. When you let go, you grow.

Let's briefly debunk a couple of other myths about forgiveness. It doesn't mean that you must resume a relationship with the offender, especially if it is very clear the person is unapologetic and has not changed their behavior. You are simply separating yourself from the hook of pain so the hurt doesn't hold you back from the life that is before you.

There is a difference between a person who hurts you by making a mistake and a person who hurts you by continuing a pattern. Mistakes can be forgiven; patterns should be broken. Forgive people in your life, even those who are not sorry for their actions. Holding on to anger only hurts you, not them.

Who hasn't been hurt by the actions or words of another? Perhaps a parent constantly criticized you growing up, or a colleague sabotaged a project, or your partner had an affair. Or maybe you've had a traumatic experience, such as being physically, sexually, or emotionally abused by someone close to you. These wounds can leave lasting feelings of resentment, bitterness, and anger... sometimes even hatred.

But if you hold on to that pain, you are the one who pays most dearly. By embracing forgiveness, you can also embrace peace and hope. Consider how forgiveness can lead you down the path of physical, emotional, and spiritual well-being.

Forgiveness means different things to different people, but in general, it involves an intentional decision to let go of resentment and anger. Forgiveness doesn't mean forgetting or excusing the harm done to you. It also doesn't necessarily mean making up with the person who caused the harm. Forgiveness brings a kind of peace that allows you to focus on yourself and helps you go on with life and possibly help others.

Letting go of grudges and bitterness can make way for improved health and peace of mind. Forgiveness can lead to:

- Healthier relationships
- Improved mental health
- Less anxiety, stress, and hostility
- Fewer symptoms of depression
- Lower blood pressure
- A stronger immune system
- Improved heart health
- Improved self-esteem

Being hurt by someone, particularly someone you love and trust, can cause anger, sadness, and confusion. If you dwell on hurtful events or situations, grudges filled with resentment and hostility can take root. If you allow negative feelings to crowd out positive feelings, you might find yourself swallowed up by bitterness or a sense of injustice.

If you struggle with finding forgiveness, you might:

- Bring anger and bitterness into new relationships and experiences
- Become so wrapped up in the wrong that you can't enjoy the present
- Become depressed, irritable, or anxious
- Feel at odds with your spiritual beliefs
- Lose valuable and enriching connections with others

Forgiveness is a commitment to change. It takes practice. To move toward forgiveness, you might:

- Recognize the value of forgiveness and how it can improve your life
- Identify what needs healing and who you want to forgive
- Join a support group or see a counselor
- Acknowledge your emotions about the harm done to you, recognize how those emotions affect your behavior, and work to release them
- Choose to forgive the person who's offended you
- Release the control and power that the offending person and situation have had in your life

Forgiveness can be hard, especially if the person who hurt you doesn't admit wrongdoing. If you find yourself stuck:

- Practice empathy
- Ask yourself about the circumstances that may have led the other person to behave in such a way
- Reflect on times when others have forgiven you
- Write in a journal and pray
- Be aware that forgiveness is a process

If the hurtful event involved someone whose relationship you valued, forgiveness may lead to reconciliation. But that isn't always the case. Reconciliation might be impossible if the offender has died or is unwilling to communicate with you. In other cases, reconciliation might not be appropriate or healthy for you. Still, forgiveness is possible—even if reconciliation isn't.

Forgiveness is about focusing on what you can control in the here and now. Think of forgiveness more about how it can change your life by bringing you peace, happiness, and emotional and spiritual healing. Forgiveness can take away the power the other person continues to have in your life.

The first step is to honestly assess and acknowledge the wrongs you've done and how they have affected others. Avoid judging yourself too harshly. If you're truly sorry for something you've said or done and want forgiveness, consider reaching out to those you've harmed. Speak of your sincere sorrow or regret. Ask for forgiveness without making excuses.

You can't force someone to forgive you. Others need to move to forgiveness in their own time. Remember, forgiveness is a process. Whatever happens, commit to treating others with compassion, empathy, and respect.

Forgiveness and reconciliation are not the same. Reconciliation is the reestablishment of a relationship and requires both people to play by the same rules. On the other hand, forgiveness is not dependent on the other person's cooperation. It's not about them; it's about you and your personal prison.

Six requirements for lasting forgiveness:

1. Decide to forgive and speak it. Mark 11:25 says: "And when you stand praying, if you hold anything against anyone, forgive them, so that your Father in heaven may forgive you your sins." (NIV)
2. Own your inner pain
3. Choose compassion
4. Find meaning in suffering
5. Create a life culture of forgiveness
6. Remove obstacles

Why is forgiveness so important?

Who do you need to forgive so you can move forward?

For if you forgive other people when they sin against you, your heavenly Father will also forgive you. (Matthew 6:14 NIV)

Suffering In Silence

Be kind to one another, tenderhearted, forgiving one another, as God in Christ forgave you. (Ephesians 4:32 ESV)

Do not take revenge, my dear friends, but leave room for God's wrath, for it is written: "It is mine to avenge; I will repay," says the Lord. (Romans 12:19 NIV)

2
Communication Is Key

Effective communication is 20 percent what you know and 80 percent how you feel about what you know. ~ Jim Rohn

Be quick to listen, be slow to speak, be slow to be offended, be slow to anger, and be conscious of making eye contact.

You've not grown up until you know how to communicate, apologize, be truthful, and accept accountability without blaming someone else. Take responsibility for your own actions!

I used to think communication was the key until I realized comprehension is. You can communicate all you want with someone, but if they don't understand you, it's silent chaos. If there's a lack of communication, there will eventually be a lack of trust due to the lack of communication.

And if there's a lack of trust, there's a real problem!!

Three simple rules to live by:

- Love needs action
- Trust needs proof
- Sorry needs change

Effective Communication:

- **Be quick to listen** – practice listening without interrupting
- **Be slow to speak** – bite your tongue and give yourself time to compose your thoughts
- **Be slow to be offended** – don't look for reasons to be offended
- **Be slow to anger** – step back and gather your thoughts before expressing yourself

Opening doors to communication:

- **Meeting and greeting** – make positive introductions, be a good listener, and if you're wearing a name tag, place it on the right shoulder
- **Making conversation** – speak wisely and listen well
- **Telephone manners** – speak clearly and use your normal tone of voice
- **Communicating with clarity and courtesy** – clarity demands the use of simple language and easy sentences; almost everything starts and ends with courtesy
- **Cyber-rules** – keep your personal information PERSONAL

Remember the old saying, "misery loves company?" Don't allow yourself to get caught up with people who are constantly negative or whose goal is to tear someone else down. Limit your time with these types of people. No one can control you unless you let them. This type of communication is not positive or beneficial to anyone.

If you are exploding, it isn't because someone pushed your buttons. It's because you pulled the trigger! Program your mind to act rather than react.

Two forms of communication:

- Non-verbal communication
- Verbal communication

Non-Verbal Communication

Wardrobe Development:

- Clothing
- Accessories
- Hair care
- Skin care
- Grooming

Body Language:

- Entrances
- Handshakes
- Eye Contact
- Territory
- Positioning

Verbal Communication

- Tone of conversation is positive
- Make good eye contact

- Verbal and non-verbal messaging is the same
- Ask questions and show interest
- Do not swear or tell off-color jokes
- Pay attention
- Show that you're a team player

Some of the factors the listener takes note of is how someone walks and what they wear. They also notice the other person's posture, gestures, facial expressions, whether they make eye contact, and what their tone of voice indicates. Being assertive verbally means very little unless your nonverbal communication supports your message. Evidence upholds the theory that the mind will respond to what the body does physically. Your two types of communication need to match. If they don't match, you are definitely sending out a very mixed message!

Communication is an area where today's society really struggles. So much of today's communication is done electronically, and you miss out on the nonverbal cues that accompanies verbal communication which tells you if their nonverbal messaging aligns with their verbal messaging. The concept of "dressing for success" is another nonverbal communication factor that has totally disappeared in society.

Sometimes the best thing you can do is keep your mouth shut and your eyes open. The truth always comes out in the end.
~ Author Unknown

What are your strengths as a communicator?

What are your weaknesses as a communicator?

A soft answer turneth away wrath: but grievous words stir up anger. (Proverbs 15:1 KJV)

There is that speaketh like the piercings of a sword: but the tongue of the wise is health. (Proverbs 12:18 KJV)

Set a watch, O LORD, before my mouth; keep the door of my lips. (Psalm 141:3 KJV)

Where's your voice

"Your voice is the most potent magic in existence."
~ Michael Bassey Johnson

"Only by speaking out can we create lasting change!"
~ DaShanne Stokes

When someone goes quiet, it's not because they have nothing to say, but because their heart is too heavy to put their pain into words. They become tired—tired of explaining, tired of being misunderstood, tired of holding it all together. Their silence isn't emptiness; it's full of emotions they can no longer express out loud. Sometimes, the deepest battles are fought in silence and the loudest cries are never heard. Don't let yourself fall into silence for any period of time!

"Where's your voice? Speak up!" is a phrase that encourages people to express themselves and stand up for what they believe in. It's not about ego. But once you feel ignored or unwanted, you distance yourself. Silently! Be proud of yourself for surviving all the silent struggles you don't speak about, but it's okay to have an opinion and you should be able to express it!

"People start to heal the moment they feel heard."
~ Cheryl Richardson

However, silence is sometimes better than saying things you will regret. Have you found yourself saying, "Don't get me started, because I don't come with brakes." Don't fuel the fire if there is one raging! There is a fine line between silence and speaking up; discernment needs to be exercised as to what is appropriate in every situation. Your peace is more important than feeling you need to confront everybody! Let them talk because none of them add value to your life.

Often the storm that was sent to break you is the storm God will use to make you. We are drowning in information these days while we are starving for wisdom at times—wisdom as to what to say and when to say it. The tongue can be very sharp, so we all need wisdom when we speak. My mom would rarely speak up for herself; she often was beat down by a number of people. She suffered dearly for her silence!

Too often we spend time looking outside ourselves for security and confidence. The truth is you have the best coach and your most loyal fan living right inside of you. It may be difficult to hear that voice of possibility at first, especially after listening to the voice of limitation for so long.

Here are some tips for finding your voice and speaking up:

- **Prepare:** Think about what you want to say and how you want to say it.

- **Practice:** Try speaking up in different situations such as with friends and family, in your community, or in your organization.
- **Build your confidence:** Work on improving your communication skills such as how you project your voice, craft a message, and listen to others.
- **Find allies:** Look for people who share your values and can support you.
- **Be authentic:** Express your unique perspective and connect with others.
- **Make an if–then plan:** Prepare for situations where you might need to speak up and develop a plan for what to say.
- **Accept your fears:** Understand why you might be afraid to speak up and then take steps to build your confidence.
- **Find a safe space:** If you're having trouble speaking up, you can consider talking to a therapist.

Despite the guilt, selfishness, and fear of disharmony speaking out may cause, the fact is that getting our needs met is fundamental to our well-being, and we can't get those needs met without using our voice. We hold back and WHY? We justify all the reasons why we should not speak up. We feel guilty or selfish. We want to maintain harmony. If a conversation goes to anger every time you speak up, it's not what you are saying but a problem with the relationship. Or we expect others to know what we need and for them to just give it to us. This can lead to exhaustion, resentment, and unhappiness.

"It took me quite a long time to develop a voice, and now that I have it, I am not going to be silent." ~ Madeleine K. Albright

Most of us feel comfortable expressing our needs when it comes to our physical health—I need food, sleep, and a walk outside. However, expressing our emotional and spiritual needs feels vulnerable. Taking this into account, there are four steps below that I feel are important in finding our voice.

> **Step 1:** Get clear about what you want and need, with tact.
> **Step 2:** Reflect on where in your life you can start asking for what you need.
> **Step 3:** Question what holds you back from asking for what you need.
> **Step 4:** Practice.

"Find your voice and inspire others to find theirs." ~ Stephen Covey

In a world where the volume of voices can drown out our own, finding the courage to speak our truth is a revolutionary act. Sometimes you can be fighting for your life, and people will notice that you aren't showing up for them the way they want. Each of us holds within us a unique perspective, a story waiting to be told. Embracing our voice is not just an act of self-expression...it's a declaration of our worthiness, our authenticity, and our right to be heard. We are all entitled to express ourselves or our opinion. We learn from each other!

As you navigate your own journey toward self-expression, remember that your voice matters. Your thoughts, your feelings, your desires— they are valid and deserving of acknowledgment. So dare to speak up, even when your voice shakes. Dare to share your truth, for it is in the sharing that we find connection, understanding, and growth.

Over time, you start losing yourself, your wants, dreams, and even your happiness because you're always putting others first. You sacrifice your time, interests, and friendships just to keep up with others' demands. It's exhausting, and you start feeling stuck and hopeless. Let your truth be heard. Let your voice resonate with the world. In doing so, you not only honor your own journey but also inspire others to find the courage to do the same. Silence is what keeps you stuck; awareness is how you begin to heal.

Speaking up when it matters can be a daunting task. It requires us to confront our fears of rejection, embarrassment, and social exclusion. Our brains are wired to avoid these negative outcomes which can make it challenging to take the first step. According to Dr. Amy Edmondson, a renowned psychologist and author, "The fear of speaking up is not just about fear of conflict or disagreement; it's also about the fear of social exclusion."

One effective way to lessen the social threat is to make it clear that you're not out to get anyone. Instead, your intention is to share your concerns or ideas to improve the situation or address a problem. This can be done by:

- Using "I" statements instead of "you" statements.
- Stating your concerns as questions rather than accusations.
- Avoiding inflammatory language and focusing on the issue at hand.
- Listening actively and responding thoughtfully to others' perspectives.

Finding your Voice is bigger and deeper than that, it's:

- HOW you show up
- Taking a stand or position on something that matters to you
- WHO you are in the workplace (and at home)
- Courage, authenticity, determination, and passion
- Connecting to your deeper WHY

When you choose silence over speaking up, or you refuse to fully show up because you are afraid, you lose. Typically, it's the voices in our heads that hold us back from finding and expressing ourselves.

How many times have these limiting thoughts played in your head?

- What if I'm wrong?
- I don't know enough!
- They're going to make fun of me.
- Who do I think I am?
- My opinion doesn't matter.
- What if I sound stupid?
- I don't want to feel like a fraud.
- If it was a good idea, someone else would have already said it.
- I don't want people to get mad at me.

One way to overcome the voice of your self-criticism is to re-frame the negative statements by flipping them around. Here are some examples:

- I wouldn't be in the room if I weren't valuable.
- I provide a different perspective.

- I know I'm genuine.
- It's okay to be wrong.
- It's okay to fail.
- My ideas are worthy of being heard.
- I can only control myself and I'm okay with that.

What is on your mind that needs to be said?

What makes you hold back from speaking up?

Even if I should choose to boast, I would not be a fool, because I would be speaking the truth. But I refrain, so no one will think more of me than is warranted by what I do or say. (2 Corinthians 12:6 NIV)

Conflict

"Conflict is inevitable, but combat is optional." ~ Max Lucado

Conflict has been viewed as a bad thing but many good things have come out of conflict. Now conflict can quickly turn into a bad thing if you don't exercise tact and respect during it. A conflict is a way to express viewpoints and offer suggestions. Everyone can learn something from a healthy conflict situation.

Most people try to avoid conflicts at all cost. The problem is people have never really learned how to communicate with each other in straightforward ways without doing damage to their relationships or without being able to negotiate their relationships so both have some room to change or some room to stay exactly the way they are. Dirty water doesn't stop plants from growing, so don't let negative words stop your progress.

Most Christians believe it is a sign of humility and godliness to suffer silently and to suppress their anger when they are hurt or offended. Suppressing your anger or frustration is unwise. While the Bible encourages peacemaking and warns against strife, Christians are also called to address issues when necessary, including confronting sin or advocating for justice. Jesus himself confronted hypocrisy and injustice, setting an example for his followers to do the same when necessary. Every repressed emotion gets expressed somewhere at some time.

People who can't communicate think everything is an argument. People who lack accountability think everything is an attack. Some people have a very low boiling point or so much repressed anger and frustration that they explode at the slightest aggravation. Obviously, this type of reaction does not fix the problem; it only makes it worse.

When you become aware that you have offended another person, it is your responsibility to work toward reconciliation. You often will sense that someone is trying to avoid you or maybe you are trying to avoid someone. Then is the time to take action in an attempt to resolve the differences.

Distance is my new answer to disrespect. I no longer react, I no longer argue, I no longer dive into drama. I simply remove myself. Remember, you teach people how to treat you by what you tolerate. Distance is not always the answer to every situation but can be the only way to deal with some of them!

We must learn to use our words effectively. Words are the tools of communication. They live on and on in people's hearts and minds. Communication is the exchange of information. To effectively resolve conflicts, we must accurately discern the root cause and be willing to listen objectively to the others person's input. This means hearing what is being said as well as what is not being said. There are many different types of personalities and temperaments. We must pause and recognize these factors before we dive head first into a conflict.

While often seen as negative, conflict can have positive aspects when managed constructively, allowing for improved communication, new ideas, and problem-solving. While negative conflict can lead to damaged relationships, decreased productivity, and emotional distress, the key is to focus on addressing issues respectfully and finding solutions that benefit everyone involved.

There are positive characteristics of conflict:

- Motivates critical thinking and innovation
- Strengthens relationships
- Personal growth
- Identifies problems early
- Promotes change
- Groupthink avoidance
- Open communication
- Respectful dialogue
- Collaboration
- Compromise

Conflict Resolution

Since conflict is a natural part of life brought on by our different beliefs, experiences, and values, turn it into collaboration conflict.

Steps adults should use to resolve conflict:

- Treat the other person with respect
- Confront the problem
- Define the conflict
- Communicate understanding
- Explore alternative solutions
- Evaluate over time
- Show interest
- Clarify
- Be patient
- Have empathy
- Talk directly to the person(s) involved
- Choose a good time to talk
- Plan ahead
- Don't blame or name-call
- Listen to all sides
- Talk it through
- Brainstorm ideas
- Look for win-win solutions
- Follow through
- Be willing to take responsibility for your actions
- Have the desire for repair

When you are asked, "Aren't you going to tell your side of the story?" just reply, "God knows and that is enough."

What would you want to feel during a conflict?

What are your goals of a conflict resolution?

A hot-tempered person stirs up conflict, but the one who is patient calms a quarrel. (Proverbs 15:18 NIV)

Assertive Communication

"Criticize less, contribute more. The world needs builders, not auditors." ~ Author Unknown

Assertive communication is a core communication skill. Being assertive can also help boost your self-esteem and earn others' respect. Because assertiveness is based on mutual respect, it's an effective and diplomatic communication style.

Being assertive means communicating positively and with conviction. It is the ability to get your message across so that it's heard and recognized. Being assertive does not mean manipulating others, being pushy, arrogant, or acting ruthless; there's enough of that in the world already.

Assertive communicators don't see themselves as better than or less than others, but as equal to. They see all parties as worthy and capable of handling a situation to best suit the needs of everyone involved. An assertive style of communication is powerful and free of judgement.

Beliefs are our own self-drawn truths based on the results of our past experiences, values, and convictions. There are no victims here!

If your tendency is to allow the needs and wants of others to determine your outcome in life, then in the long run you will find yourself angry and depressed throughout life. Who you are on the outside is a direct reflection of what's going on inside, so guard your thoughts.

It's not just what you say – your message – but also how you say it that's important. Assertive communication is direct and respectful. If you communicate in a way that's too passive or too aggressive, your message may get lost because people will be too busy reacting to your delivery.

Being prepared to be assertive includes the following:

- Engaging in mental preparation – get your thoughts in order
- Creating a supportive environment – find a mutual place
- Using good timing – timing is everything

The secret to managing your mouth is to start by managing your head. While of course there are times when you're caught off guard, very often you do have time to prepare for your interactions.

How does one prepare for "the conversation":

- Short- and long-term goals for the conversation
- Your assumptions
- The behavior you're having a problem with, not the personal traits

- What you want from the person
- Why the person would benefit from changing the behavior

"I'll do whatever the group decides." Does this sound familiar? If so, you tend to avoid conflict. Why is that a problem? Because the message you're sending is that your thoughts and feelings aren't as important as those of other people. In essence, when you're too passive, you give others the license to disregard your wants and needs.

Being assertive is usually viewed as a healthier communication style. Being assertive offers many benefits. It helps you keep people from walking all over you. By becoming more assertive, you can begin to express your true feelings and needs more easily. You may even find you get more of what you want as a result.

Assertive communication must be direct, specific, and offer a solution. The average person only uses 3 percent of their total capabilities; assertive effective communication is a great way to expand those capabilities. Also, watch the tone of voice you are using. An incorrect tone of voice can be threatening to some.

If you allow your doubts and fears to get in your way, they will. You have two choices: allow things to go on as usual and accept the consequences of your behavior, or try a new behavior and open up the possibility for a new response. Taking responsibility for and assertively expressing your feelings is always the best way to go.

Remember that the formula for assertive behavior is based on creating win-win agreements. Be prepared to point out how both you and others will benefit from the changes made. Stay away from people who think you're arguing every time you try to express yourself.

Preparing for a meaningful assertive conversation:

- Choose a neutral place
- Speak with the person privately
- Pick a time when you both can be fully engaged and not distracted

DON'T:

- Have the conversation in front of other people unless they are directly involved
- Continue the conversation if the other person seems to be distracted
- Sit with a desk or table between you so the other person doesn't feel threatened
- Interrupt the other person; let them speak

Communicate your thoughts and feelings calmly and directly without blaming others. Don't offer your interpretation and assumptions as a fact. It is crucial to recognize that the real issue lies not in the emotions we experience, but in our responses and the methods we use to convey those feelings to others. Most of us struggle with honoring our own values. We choose our actions in hopes of winning the praise and recognition of others, and then blame them for the negative consequences of our actions. Every time you say "no" to someone or something, you are saying "yes" to someone or something else.

The Negative Consequences of Poor Communication

- Depression
- Resentment
- Frustration/physical complaints
- Temper/violence
- Anxiety/avoidance
- Poor relationships/parenting problems

Experts report that when you speak, 93 percent of your listener's interpretation has to do with everything but what you are saying. The listener makes decisions about the accuracy of the information, how trustworthy you are, and many other things based on the delivery of your message rather than on the content.

What are the underlying issues or factors contributing to the conflict?

Everyone should be quick to listen, slow to speak and slow to become angry. (James 1:19 NIV)

3

Forms of Abuse

Verbal

"The scars you can't see are the hardest to heal." ~ Astrid Alauda

When life gets heavy, remind yourself,
you're stronger than you think.

Verbal abuse is the regular, ongoing use of harmful words or a sharp tone in an attempt to control or dominate another person. Abuse means mistreatment, the destructive misuse of something or someone. Verbal abuse is always destructive. Besides verbal abuse being destructive, it is often used to hurt the reputation of others. It uses tactics such as backbiting, belittling talk, and strategies such as slander, slurs, and lies.

Many people fail to recognize that they are in an abusive relationship because abuse has been their "normal" for so long. Any form of abuse is abuse. Often people who are verbal abusers will say "Don't wear your feelings on your sleeve," or "Don't be so touchy!" Many in my family now recognize we were raised with a fair amount of verbal abuse. Some of the phrases we commonly heard were "You'll never amount to anything," "You're fat," or "You're dumb!" Unfortunately, our mom endured an immense amount of verbal abuse for years and didn't even know it until her later years because it was so common.

Those who seek to control or to overpower you with verbal attacks may not be as strong and self-assured as they appear. If they express inappropriate anger toward you, realize that their attacks are not about you, but about them. When people can't control you, they try to control how people VIEW you. After all of the years of control, when my dad passed away, my mom had to learn to think for herself because she was never allowed to. At the age of 69, every decision was a very difficult one for her. It was a new way of life she was not familiar with.

How do you break the cycle of an abusive relationship?

1. State very clearly, in a conversation or a letter, what you are willing to accept and not accept from the abuser.
2. Announce the consequences you will enforce if the abuser violates your requests.
3. Enforce the consequences every single time the abuse occurs.
4. Absolutely do not negotiate.
5. Never "react" when your boundary is violated—only respond.
6. Solicit the support of one or two wise, objective people to help you through this process.

What triggers the verbal abuse, and how does it escalate?

Emotional and Psychological

Emotional abuse eventually brainwashes the victim!

"We stumble over pebbles, never over mountains." ~ Marilyn French

"You cannot solve a problem until you acknowledge that you have one and accept responsibility for solving it." ~ Zig Ziglar

Emotional abuse is any ongoing, negative behavior used to control or hurt another person. Emotional abuse ranges from consistent indifference to continual belittling of a character.

Abuse isn't always physical; it's also ABUSE, if...

- You experience constant criticism that focuses on your character, personality, or things you can't change.
- You aren't allowed to make your own choices or say no without unpleasant consequences.
- You're walking on eggshells constantly, monitoring your behavior to avoid angering, triggering, or disappointing the other person.
- You feel like you can't relax or be yourself without negative consequences.
- The other person withdraws love, affection, or respect in order to punish or control you.
- The other person accuses you of things that aren't true or things they're doing.

- The goalposts constantly move; no matter how much you try to meet the other person's expectations, it's not enough. The rules keep changing or demands keep increasing.
- The other person isolates you from loved ones. They criticize them, discouraging activities, then guilt trip you or call or text relentlessly when you're with them.
- You're expected to always be there for them and validate and soothe them. But your achievements or struggles are belittled or dismissed.

Trauma says: I should have done things differently. Healing says: hindsight offers clarity, but I did the best I could with what I knew at the time. I deserve to be gentle with myself even when I make mistakes.

If you alter your behavior because you are frightened of how your partner will react, you are being abused. Never respond to insults. The main purpose of an insulter is to make you act without thinking. Frustrate them with your silence. This is a situation where silence can be beneficial. Never forget: you are a limited edition. There's no one like you! Love should not leave you traumatized. Whatever happened to you was not love if it left you traumatized.

I used to take other people's behavior personally. But now I understand that how I show up is a reflection of me, and how others show up is a reflection of them. What they project has more to do with what's going on inside of them than it does with me, and vice versa.

One red flag of an emotional abuser is that they use blame shifting to escape accountability. They treat you badly, act disrespectfully, verbally abuse you, and then focus on your reaction, claiming you are unstable, responsible for how you feel, or that you need professional help. Feeling hurt, angry, and upset is completely normal reactions to feelings of being abused or someone being rude or cruel. What is not normal is the toxic person shifting the blame to you instead of apologizing, showing remorse, or taking accountability.

"Just because you grew up a certain way doesn't mean you have to stay stuck in those habits. You're an adult now, and you have the power to make changes." ~ Author Unknown

Hurting someone and expecting them to move on like nothing happened is emotional abuse. Someone who destroys your mental health cannot be the love of your life. Some of the damage from emotional abuse manifests as: feeling a deep sense of unworthiness, a continuous feeling of anxiety, inadequacy, inferiority, an inner nagging that says, "I'm not good enough, I'll never amount to anything. No one could ever possibly love me. Everything I do is wrong."

We were raised with emotional abuse, but we didn't know that was what it was at the time. We just knew we could never do anything right for our father. My one sister and I were told we would never amount to anything and were too dumb to do anything more than dishes at our local café.

Emotional abuse is the unseen fallout of all other forms of abuse: physical, mental, verbal, sexual, and even spiritual abuse. People often minimize the importance of emotions. Yet for deeply wounded people, their feelings can be the driving force behind their choices, the life-sustaining element of their very beings. Emotional abuse strikes at the very core of what we are, crushing our confidence, wearing away our sense of worth, crushing our spirit. Emotional abuse is often the root cause of suicide.

The abuser takes control of the victim's time and physical environment and works to suppress much of the victim's old behavior. The victim is slowly, or abruptly, isolated from all supportive people except the abuser/brainwasher. An abuser will make their victim feel powerless, fearful, and dependent on them. Sometimes you can be fighting for your life, and people will notice that you aren't showing up for them the way they want. It's all about them!

Dark times teach you a lot. That's why you can't regret what you went through but rather be thankful for all the lessons it taught you. One of the most devastating forms of abuse is when your suffering is not recognized – when people make you believe that you are the problem while they are mistreating you. ~ Author Unknown

One big question is does abuse justify divorce? This is a very difficult question to answer, but let's look at a few facts and scriptures regarding this subject. Many people immediately point to the scripture in Malachi 2:16:

"The man who hates and divorces his wife," says the LORD, the God of Israel, "does violence to the one he should protect," says the LORD Almighty. So be on your guard, and do not be unfaithful.

This scripture addresses violence and unfaithful husbands. Restoration of an abusive relationship should be approached cautiously. Forgiveness does not mean tolerating ongoing abuse.

God's heart is for justice and freedom, and He desires for all to live in peace and safety.

An abusive spouse, in fact, has abandoned the marriage. Abuse is much worse than abandonment, involving the misuse of something holy, marriage. Sometimes the one being abused will believe that there is no other option but to stay, feeling trapped in the marriage. In the case of domestic violence, the church has a responsibility not only to alert the authorities but also to bear the abuse sufferer's burdens by arranging a safe place for refuge for those in need. Divorce for domestic violence is not a sin. It's about sin all right, but it's the sin of the abuser, not the sin of the abused who decides to divorce.

These biblical principles help guide our response to abuse:

1. **Prioritize safety** – the Bible supports seeking safety and protecting you and your children from harm.
2. **Seek justice** – Proverbs 31:8-9 encourages speaking up for those who cannot speak for themselves (children), highlighting the importance of justice and advocacy.
3. **Offer empathy and support** – Romans 12:15 instructs believers to rejoice with those who rejoice and to mourn with those who mourn.
4. **Understand the role of forgiveness** – forgiveness involves releasing personal bitterness, while safety and well-being must be prioritized.
5. **Encourage genuine change** – true restoration requires significant change in the abuser's behavior.

The damage from emotional abuse lasts far longer than damage from any other kind of abuse. After extended periods of emotional abuse, many victims lose hope, feeling that life is not worth living. Sometimes emotional abuse can be a passive-aggressive tactic. Passive-aggressive abuse is a means of indirect, underhanded control. A passive aggressive abuser often uses manipulation as a means of making the abused feel responsible for the abuser's emotional and physical well-being. The abuser then becomes very critical of everything the abused tries to do to make them happy.

Silent Treatment:

- Is emotionally abusive
- Is used as a control tactic
- Confuses the victim
- Causes anxiety for the victim
- Crushes a victim's self-esteem
- Is a form of manipulation

The best way to confront and cope with emotionally abusive people:

1. **Educate yourself** – abusers can be calculating, and their behavior may be deliberate and designed to keep you in control.
2. **Set boundaries** – communicate that you will not be treated with disrespect.
3. **Get ahold of the moment** – speak up as soon as the abuser begins to change the subject or to twist your words

around to mean something other than what you intended. Remain calm! Your abuser wants a strong reaction from you.

4. **Get the other person to discuss their hostility** – acknowledge that you sense the anger in the other person.

5. **Soften the confrontation process** – confront the behavior, not the person.

6. **Stay in the present** – focus on the issue at hand and don't let the other person get you off track.

7. **Crush unrealistic expectations** – be aware that you cannot make the abuser change no matter what you do, how much you try, or how good you are as a person. Know that change will occur only after the abuser admits to having a problem.

8. **Strengthen your relationship with the Lord** – look to the Lord for discernment about the relationship.

There are four phases to emotional abuse:

Phase 1 – Tension increases, communication is broken

Phase 2 – Verbal and emotional abuse, anger, blaming, arguing, intimidation

Phase 3 – Abuser apologizes, gives excuses, and denies abuse

Phase 4 – Calm, incident forgotten, no abuse right now

Verbally abusing a woman hurts just as much as hitting her. Bruises fade away, but words leave a scar that doesn't heal. Sometimes things that break your heart end up fixing your vision. When life gets heavy, remind yourself that you're stronger than you think. When God takes out the trash, don't go dumpster diving to bring it back.

One of the most devastating forms of abuse is when you're suffering is not recognized—when people make you believe that you are the problem all the while they are mistreating you. Nobody's perfect, but they should not try to flip the script and make your reactions the issue when their actions lit the match! Reactive abuse happens when someone pushes you until you act out of character. Then, they shame you for reacting. If you hold a match to a candle, sooner or later, it will start to burn.

So many people have been conditioned to believe that abuse is only "real" if it leaves physical scars. But that is a dangerous lie. Abuse doesn't have to come in the form of punches, kicks, or bruises to destroy a person's life. They don't have to hit you, choke you, or slam your head into a wall in order for it to be domestic violence. The truth is, abuse has many faces, and most of them don't leave visible marks.

It's in the way they degrade you with cruel words until you start doubting your own worth. It's in the way they humiliate you in front of others to break down your confidence. It's in the way they scream, yell, and twist your emotions until you're left walking on eggshells, terrified of their next explosion. It's the constant blame-shifting, where somehow every problem is made to seem like it's your fault. It's in the endless lies, betrayals, and cheating that chip away at your sense of security and stability.

You cannot see your reflection in boiling water. Similarly, you cannot see the truth in a state of anger. When the water calms, clarity comes. Healing doesn't mean the damage never existed. It means the damage no longer controls your life.

You are not defined by the storms you face but by the light you carry through the storm. Your kindness, resilience and hope make you unbreakable and even when the winds blow, your spirit whispers: "I will not be moved, I will rise stronger than ever."

A woman who gets her strength from God can never be broken. No matter how big the storm is today, remember four things:

1. The Lord shall fight for you (Exodus 14:14)
2. Be still, and know that I am God (Psalm 46:10)
3. But they that wait on the Lord shall renew their strength (Isaiah 40:31)
4. I will never leave you, nor forsake you (Hebrews 13:5)

Just because a person doesn't put hands on you, doesn't mean they are not abusive. Abuse is control, blatant disrespect, and also hurtful words. Don't settle for emotional abuse thinking it's okay because it's not physical.

Sometimes you'll spend a lifetime untangling the knots that you did not tie. ~ JM Storm

Emotional maturity is letting people be wrong about you. It's understanding their narrative has nothing to do with who you are. Maintain self control and never reply when you're angry. Never make a promise when you're happy. Never make a decision when you're sad.

I don't wish harm upon anyone, but one reaps what they sow in life. You don't treat people badly and live a happy life. When they can't compete with your character, they attack on your reputation. You can't mistreat people and then act like they betrayed you. That's delusional.

A woman never forgets how a man treated her during the times she needed his support the most. I don't think women are becoming heartless. I think they are becoming more aware of what they deserve and how they want to be treated. Having to beg someone to do something with you and then seeing them do it with others willingly is a different kind of heartbreak.

And if you're someone from the outside looking in, I encourage you to think before you choose sides without knowing the full and true story of a situation. You might be surprised about how sneaky some people are by causing trouble and then playing the victim.

If you constantly have to tell someone the exact same thing about how you feel and they don't change, understand they don't respect you.

Signs of emotional abuse:

- **Humiliation, degradation, discounting, negating, judging, and criticizing:** Does anyone make fun of you or put you down in front of others? Does anyone regularly ridicule, dismiss, and disregard your opinions, thoughts, suggestions, and feelings?
- **Domination, control, and shame:** Do they treat you as though you are inferior to them? Do they make you feel as though they are always right?
- **Accusing and blaming, trivial and unreasonable demands or expectations, denial of their own shortcomings:** Do they make excuses for their behavior or tend to blame others for the circumstance of their mistakes? Do they blame you for their problems or unhappiness?

- **Emotional distancing and the "silent treatment," isolation, emotional abandonment, or neglect:** Do they use pouting, withdrawal, or withholding attention or affection? Do they play the victim to deflect blame onto you instead of taking responsibility for their actions and attitudes?
- **Codependence and enmeshment:** Do they disrespect your requests and do what they think is best for you? Does anyone treat you not as a separate person but instead as an extension of themselves?

Things you must do to heal from your damaged emotions:

- Face your problem squarely and honestly
- Accept your responsibility in the matter
- Identify the REAL problem
- Ask yourself if you want your wounds to heal so you can move on
- Forgive everyone who is involved in your problem
- Forgive yourself

Self-confidence is extremely important in almost every aspect of our lives, yet many people struggle to find it. Many people have been beaten down so many times, they have no self-confidence left in them. People who lack self-confidence can find it difficult to become successful. The good news is that self-confidence can be learned and built on.

Self-confidence comes not from always being right but from not fearing to be wrong. ~ Peter T. Mcintyre

God is saying to you today, "I know you are physically drained, but you have to keep going. I'll see you through. You're going to make it. You and your family will be just fine. Just stand and let Me fight this battle."

Where do you currently feel most confident?

Where do you struggle with confidence?

I can do all things through Christ who strengthens me.
(Philippians 4:13 NKJV)

For God has not given us a spirit of fear, but of power and of love and of a sound mind. (2 Timothy 1:7 NKJV)

Therefore do not cast away your confidence, which has great reward. For you have need of endurance, so that after you have done the will of God, you may receive the promise...
(Hebrews 10:35–36 NKJV)

Manipulative – Narcissist – Control

"Nobody can be kinder than the narcissist while you react to life in his own terms." ~ Elizabeth Bowen

"Things come apart so easily when they have been held together with lies." ~ Dorothy Allison

Manipulation

What exactly is manipulation? Manipulation is the art of controlling people or circumstances by indirect, unfair, or deceptive means, especially if it is to one's own advantage. Manipulation happens when people allow others to control them excessively. So then, what is persuasion? It is the act of convincing others by urging, reasoning, and appealing to their minds. Persuasion is a process of winning others by logical facts. Don't get these two confused—those who manipulate use dishonest emotions to achieve their goal while those who persuade use honest reason to achieve their goal.

To be manipulated is to allow another person to dictate your thoughts, feelings, and behaviors. It is also others making decisions for you and others having control over you. Some use a verbal method of playing their game and others use a nonverbal method of manipulation.

Manipulation is when others blame you for your reaction to their toxic behavior but never discuss the disrespect that triggered you. The reason why these people don't see anything wrong with their behavior and how they treat you is because they are surrounded by enablers that are okay with it. It's not just one person; it's an army of people that encourage this. The difference between them and you is that you didn't have to twist the story to make the other person look bad; they accomplished that all on their own!

What is the background of manipulation and where does it come from? As a child you may have had an over-controlling parent who was domineering, critical, angry, or manipulative. Sometimes it comes from abuse as a child: verbal emotional, physical, and sexual. Maybe you simply had no voice as a child. Your feelings and viewpoint didn't matter! Some children accept the blame for everything in childhood; this is a mindset that will position you up to be manipulated as an adult.

Typically, the manipulated don't understand why they can so easily be manipulated. Some people are truly great manipulators. They can lie, cheat, treat you badly, and somehow manage to make it all seem like your fault. Don't fall for it... that is just what they do.

Generally, there is a combination of misbeliefs:

- **Misplaced dependence** – I must have you in my life
- **Misplaced priorities** – the judgement and opinion of others
- **Fear of disapproval** – fear of making someone upset
- **Performance-based acceptance** – concerned about pleasing others
- **Defensive about their relationships** – can't see that the relationship is unhealthy
- **Loss of independence** – feel guilty if they want alone time
- **Loss of confidence** – made to believe they make poor decisions or their memory is wrong
- **Loss of identity** – controlled by the manipulator's personality or power
- **Loss of objectivity** – makes excuses for the manipulator

Often a manipulator will control their victim through brainwashing. There is both verbal and emotional brainwashing, and many manipulators use both types at the same time! Verbal brainwashing is intimidation, indoctrination, discrediting, degrading or labeling.

Emotional brainwashing is isolation, excessive compliance, ignoring, or exploiting.

Manipulation is when someone repeatedly promises to meet your needs but never delivers. Forgive yourself for falling into their trap, because a good heart often fails to see the bad. You deserve people who won't let you down and break your heart over and over again. Be prepared for rejection when you refuse to be manipulated.

"Some people will never have the courage to face the fact that they hurt you. Instead of owning up to their actions, they'll create false stories to protect their ego and avoid feeling guilty. It's not about you, it's about their inability to take responsibility..."
~ Author Unknown

Sometimes we have to remind ourselves we are not responsible for other people's poor behavior towards us, or their gaslighting, or their manipulation, or their unkindness. That's on them. What's on you is how you choose to respond, set boundaries, know your worth, and not let their actions impact the beautiful soul that you are.

Some people will go to great lengths to provoke you out of your normal character so they can put blame on you rather than themselves. Chances are that they created a narrative about you and they need you to act on it to prove their innocence. Please don't fall into this trap.

Things to remember when recovering from abuse:

1) **Self-compassion** – acknowledge that healing takes time
Set small achievable goals. No matter how small your goal
may be that you achieve, acknowledge a win.

2) **Surround yourself with supportive people** – seek out
people who nurture and respect you. Connect with people
who are positive and have like interests.

Narcissist

What is a narcissistic personality? Narcissistic personality disorder is
a mental health condition that manifests in these ways and more:

1. A person with an inflated sense of their own value or worth
2. Lack of empathy
3. Needs constant and excessive admiration
4. Behaves in an arrogant fashion
5. Difficulty in forming relationships
6. Takes advantage of other people, especially if it will help
   them achieve their goal
7. Believes they are more special than anyone else
8. Requires excessive admiration

A covert narcissist is an individual with narcissistic personality
disorder (NPD) whose grandiosity and entitlement are hidden behind
a façade of shyness, humility, or insecurity, which makes them appear
introverted and self-conscious rather than overly boastful. They use
subtle manipulation like passive-aggressiveness and victim playing to

gain admiration and control, often causing confusion and emotional exhaustion to those around them.

A key indicator that you're in a narcissistic relationship is when things only remain peaceful as long as you suppress your feelings, thoughts, and opinions. A narcissist will bluntly lie directly to your face while you have proof in hand and then get mad at you for questioning and not trusting them.

Take note—after a break up, the loyal ones take time to heal and reflect while the narcissist quickly finds someone new to fill the void and feed their ego. Good people fall for narcissists not because they don't spot red flags, but because it is difficult for them to believe that someone who claims to love them can be so hurtful! Narcissists don't discard you for someone better. They discard you for someone who can't see through their lies. Narcissists don't heal...they replace. They run from accountability by running to someone new.

Men are 40 percent more likely to be diagnosed with narcissistic personality disorder than women. Both men and women who are narcissists seek attention; however, men are more prone to entitlement and violence. Women are more prone to emotional manipulation and self-absorption. Just because you don't see narcissistic traits in a person does not mean that they do not exist.

Narcissists are not in counseling to work on themselves or change. If they go to any type of counseling, they are in counseling to look good and pass the blame of a failed relationship onto the other person. Narcissists believe that because they are above the rules, they can use any means they choose such as:

- Violence
- Exploitation
- Manipulation
- Scheming
- Shaming
- Ignoring boundaries
- Being two-faced
- Deception

Wisdom will save you from evil people, from those whose words are twisted. These men turn from the right way to walk down dark paths. They take pleasure in doing wrong, and they enjoy the twisted ways of evil. (Proverbs 2: 12-14 NLT)

Narcissists will disguise themselves and are very secretive. They don't want to appear as a wolf; they want to appear gentle and unassuming. Their tactics include:

- Subtle disrespect
- Undermining authority
- Being intentionally misleading
- Withholding information
- Shaming
- Guilt-tripping
- Minimizing feelings
- Questioning motives
- Nitpick values
- Withholding affection
- Withholding money

- Mind games
- Challenging character
- Playing the "devoted servant" card

Narcissists see people as objects. They say all the right things to avoid consequences, but they will never follow through with their actions. Those words don't mean nearly as much as changed behavior. Narcissists may express pain, but it is never sadness for pain they have caused another person. It is only sorrow for the pain that they are in. When someone is truly sorry for the pain they have caused, they will seek to make amends, not excuses.

A narcissist is someone who demands you give up everything in order to be their nothing. Narcissists hate anyone who reveals the truth about them. Exposure is their biggest fear. Narcissists aren't sorry they hurt you. They're sorry they got caught! Emotion for a narcissist equates to fuel. They want to hear you getting irritated. They want to see you getting annoyed. They want to hear your voice rise and see the tears of frustration welling up in your eyes. When they see and hear this, it makes them feel so powerful.

Narcissists will deliberately neglect their parental duties and will make false claims that you're the one alienating the children from them. What makes a narcissist worse is their obsession with wanting to appear good. They will cause so much destruction and then act like the victims of the circumstances they have created.

"Narcissists Love Control! Take yours back! Stop explaining yourself...They don't actually want to understand you. They want control. Stop waiting for them to admit they're wrong...they won't.

Suffering In Silence

Focus on your own healing. Stop trying to prove your worth to them...they already know your worth. They just want you to question it." ~ Henry Cloud

Narcissists say they hate drama while they are the ones creating it. Narcissists can't handle the truth. Any mention of the truth will result in rage, deflection, projection, or gaslighting. Whenever a narcissist posts on social media, it usually involves that rage, gaslighting, or projection. They make the post all about themselves and their target is always shown in a terrible light. If you're the victim of a narcissist's post, don't let it send you spiraling!

They control you by slowly conditioning you to do what they want. If you don't abide by their rules, they will punish you. They don't necessarily tell you that. They groom you slowly and subtly to accept their rules. Before you know it, you avoid doing things you would normally enjoy doing.

Narcissists don't feel guilty for cheating on their partner. Instead, they believe that cheating is an acceptable way to deal with their own unhappiness and they rationalize it by blaming their partners for it. Narcissists claim their exes are crazy, as it's easier than admitting they cheated on them repeatedly, lied to them daily, gaslit them constantly, bankrupted them financially, took away all their friends and family, controlled them by using force, hurt them emotionally, and then abandoned them once they'd drained them completely.

Manipulators hate people who ask questions because truth destroys the games they play in silence. When you are in a relationship with a narcissist, there is always a whole secret life going on behind your back.

Narcissists make their children feel responsible for their emotions. The child fears that rejecting the narcissist will "hurt" them, make them angry, or trigger abandonment. The narcissist pits the child against the other parent, framing them as the "difficult" or "unstable" parent. The child, confused and desperate for approval, absorbs this false narrative. A narcissistic parent doesn't raise children; they raise lifelong sources of supply. They guilt-trip, manipulate, and demand loyalty while offering none in return. A narcissist won't fight for their children; they'll fight for control, attention, and the appearance of being involved and a good parent.

Cutting off a narcissist from your life and radically accepting you are going to be the villain in their delusional world is top-level self-care. Again, when God takes the trash out of your life, don't go dumpster diving to bring it back!

Narcissists only surround themselves with people who enable their behavior, ignore their behavior, or encourage their behavior. Anyone who tries to hold them accountable will be accused and blamed of the exact things the narcissist is guilty of doing. And the people who know the truth will remain silent.

When divorcing a narcissist, they completely dismiss any of your needs or all the years of devotion and support you built together. For the narcissist, it's all gone, like it never happened. They will undermine you with your friends and your children and steal all your money, if possible, all the while acting and looking sincere and generating goodwill among the community. Stay alert and watch your back to enable a better future.

A person who can consciously hurt you, lie about you, and try to destroy your credibility knowing very well that you are trustworthy is a person with no conscience. And a person with no conscience is a very dangerous person. It's hard to determine what they might do!

Remember, a narcissist always sees themselves as the victim no matter how horribly they've treated someone else. Again, the problem is not their lying, cheating, stealing, and abuse. The problem is when you start to notice those things.

A narcissist has two sets of rules. They demand you do all the apologizing. YOU have to respect them, YOU can't say anything or criticize them, YOU do whatever they say, and YOU can't have feelings or express those feelings. However, none of those rules apply to them. They can do and say whatever they want, whenever they want, never apologize, be totally disrespectful, and they seem to think it's perfectly fine.

Narcissists live a double life. They will secure a partner, all the while having another one on the side. Narcissists do this because they don't like to be alone and want to make sure they have a backup plan in case one relationship doesn't work out!

Pay close attention to the narcissist's accusations because more often than not, they're not telling you about "you." They're revealing themselves. This is called "projection"—a psychological defense mechanism where someone attributes their own unacceptable behaviors, feelings, or intentions to someone else. And narcissists are masters at it. They don't just lie to others. They lie to themselves too. But deep down, they know who they really are—and instead of facing that truth, they deflect it onto the people closest to them.

So, when they call you a liar, it's because they are the ones who have been lying. When they accuse you of cheating, it's often because they are the ones who have been unfaithful. When they say you're manipulative, dramatic, or toxic, what they're really doing is describing themselves.

It's not about your actions—it's about their guilt, their shame, and their fear of being exposed. And rather than confront that inner darkness, they try to make you carry it. They want you confused, constantly second-guessing yourself, and apologizing for things you didn't even do.

But once you learn the pattern, you begin to see the truth...

Every accusation is a mirror.

Every angry outburst, every passive-aggressive jab, every twisted story they tell about you is really a reflection of themselves—their behavior, their mindset, their hidden intentions.

The accusations aren't just lies, they're actually confessions, clumsy attempts to avoid accountability by projecting their brokenness onto you. So, the next time a narcissist throws blame your way, don't internalize it. Decode it. In their desperate effort to hide who they really are, they're actually telling you everything you need to know.

Being raised by a narcissist father means your father hasn't fully matured emotionally. His main focus is his own needs, the way he's perceived by others, and being "respected" by his family. He tends to confuse respect with obedience. He doesn't want connection, vulnerability, or emotional closeness—he wants control. He expects to be admired and followed without question, even if his actions are hurtful or unfair. Expressing your feelings or setting boundaries is seen as disrespect. In his world, love is conditional. If you agree with him, you are praised. If you challenge him, you are punished—emotionally, mentally, or even through cold silence.

Growing up like this teaches you to suppress your voice. You walk on eggshells, constantly calculating your words and actions to avoid triggering his ego. You learn to doubt yourself, to prioritize his moods over your own peace, and to shrink yourself so you don't outshine him. Your achievements may be ignored or claimed to be his own, while your mistakes are magnified and used against you.

A narcissistic father doesn't guide or nurture. He dominates and invalidates. He's more concerned with how the family appears in public than how they feel in private. Your emotional needs are dismissed as weakness and empathy is rarely shown. Over time, this creates deep wounds as well as feelings of unworthiness, people-pleasing tendencies, and a longing for a father who truly sees and supports you. Healing begins when you recognize that his behavior was not your burden to carry and you start reclaiming your identity, one truth at a time.

Narcissists, contrary to popular belief, do not choose their victims primarily because they are weak or vulnerable. They choose them mainly for the admirable strengths and qualities that they lack. Those qualities include such things as empathy, kindness, or competence. They are drawn to these qualities because they see them as a source of attention and validation.

They see it as a challenge to conquer us. They get sick pleasure out of it. A narcissist will never see an ex as the "one who got away." Their mindset doesn't allow for regret over losing someone good. Instead, they convince themselves that the person was never good enough for them in the first place. In their eyes, it's always the other person who fell short, not them.

When narcissists appear to have changed for their new partner, it's because they have. Narcissists change with every new partner to match the type of person the new partner will desire the most. These aren't real changes and are only an act before the weakening of the victim begins.

The simple truth is that narcissists cannot change. They can only wear different masks. A narcissist will never feel empathy or remorse for what they do to you. A narcissist will set you on fire and blame you for burning. Narcissists don't have partners, they have hostages.

Narcissists don't co-parent; they counter parent. They don't care about collateral damage done to the children as long as it hurts the other parent. A widely circulated sentiment in the narcissist abuse recovery community goes something like this: A narcissistic parent will fight tooth and nail over the kids, but never for the kids. For them, it's never been for the kids, never is for the kids, never will be for the kids. It's all for themselves."

One of the clearest signs that you have a narcissist in your life is if you approach them about something they did that hurt you and they get mad. A person who can't answer your questions without getting angry or defensive is hiding more than just the answer.

They don't dislike you because you did something wrong. They dislike you because you see them for who they are. You see the manipulation, the lies, the way they twist the truth, and the way they play the victim.

A narcissistic man usually has a mother wound. They could have been rejected by their mother, neglected emotionally, or conversely, they may have been the golden child—idealized, overpraised, and molded to meet their mother's unmet needs. In either case, the relationship dynamic becomes deeply damaging. The rejected son learns early that love is conditional and often develops a hardened, self-protective ego to mask his feelings of unworthiness. The golden child, on the other hand, may enjoy the praise and attention but silently suffers under the weight of emotional entrapment, growing up in a home where his identity is not truly his own. The dominating mother's affection feels smothering, not nurturing, and over time, it weakens him, creating a deep resentment he may not even consciously recognize.

Most narcissists are not aware of this mother wound, but it runs like an invisible thread throughout their adult relationships. They unconsciously seek to resolve the original trauma by recreating the same dynamics with their partners. This is where you come in. You unknowingly become a stand-in for his mother. Whether he idealizes you or degrades you, he is not truly seeing you for who you are. Instead, he projects his unresolved pain onto you. One day you're his savior, the next you're the source of all his suffering. He might charm, manipulate, or gaslight you. These are all tactics designed to maintain control and suppress the terror of abandonment or the shame of inadequacy rooted in childhood.

Over time, you will begin to feel the emotional toll of this projection. There will be confusion, exhaustion, self-doubt, and an ever-growing sense that something isn't right. This isn't love; it's trauma reenactment. Healing from such a relationship requires understanding the depth of this pattern, reclaiming your sense of self, and often grieving not just the relationship but the illusion it represented.

Predictable Narcissistic Behaviors:

All narcissists have the same patterns of behavior. One behavior they use is manipulation, especially when it comes to your feelings and trying to worm their way out of accountability. When you confront a narcissist about how he/she treats you or makes you feel, instead of sincerely apologizing or reflecting on their actions, they quickly shift the conversation away from what they did and focus it back onto you. They often use dismissive, gaslighting language designed to invalidate your emotions and confuse your sense of reality. Common phrases they use are:

- "You're too sensitive."
- "You need to move on."
- "Get over it."
- "Quit hanging on to it."
- "Let it go."
- "You misunderstood."
- "You're overanalyzing."
- "You're just paranoid."
- "You think everyone is out to get you."

This manipulative tactic serves multiple purposes. It puts you on the defensive, makes you question your own reactions, and subtly shames you for even bringing up the issue. Over time, this can eat away at your confidence and sense of self-worth, making you more dependent on the narcissist and less likely to challenge their behavior in the future. They turn themselves into the victim or the misunderstood party while painting you as unreasonable, irrational, or overly emotional.

It's a clever psychological strategy, one that is used not just occasionally, but systematically. This is how narcissists maintain power and control in relationships. They minimize your experiences, invalidate your emotions, and avoid any real accountability. The goal is not peace or understanding but control and self-protection. Once you recognize this cycle, it becomes easier to detach, set boundaries, and reclaim your sense of truth and emotional autonomy.

Narcissists don't choose losers. They want fantastic people who make them look good, or from whom they can extract some kind of benefit—status, admiration, attention, resources, or emotional supply. So if you were chosen by a narcissist, it wasn't by accident or out of pity.

It was deliberate.

You were selected because of the good in you. Your intelligence, your empathy, your confidence, your charm, your resilience, your accomplishments—those were all things they found desirable. You were chosen because you shine. You were chosen because you had something they didn't. And that's exactly where the tragedy begins.

At first, they admire those qualities. They even put you on a pedestal, making you feel special and valued. But it never lasts. Narcissists are deeply insecure and frequently annoyed. The same traits that initially drew them to you become sources of torment for them. They begin to resent your strength, your goodness, your joy. They hate that you had a fulfilling life before them, that you're capable of happiness they can't manufacture, that people love you genuinely while they must manipulate affection.

This is why you feel confused, why love seems to turn into disrespect. It's not about you being unworthy, but rather it's about them being unable to tolerate your worth. A narcissist doesn't care about BEING a good person, They are obsessed with APPEARING like a good person to everyone.

Rules of a Narcissist:

Do as I say, not as I do – Double standards aren't a flaw in my world, they're the foundation. I demand perfection from you, but I'm free to act without accountability. My actions are never up for question, but yours will be scrutinized under a microscope.

I'm never wrong – I don't apologize. I don't reflect. I rewrite reality to make myself the victim or the hero, never the villain. If you challenge me, prepare to be gaslit until you question your own sanity. I'll shift blame so expertly that you'll wonder if you started the fire I lit.

It's my way or the highway – Compromise is weakness. Obedience is loyalty. Disagree with me, and you'll feel the freeze of silence, the sting of rage, or the sudden withdrawal of affection. You're allowed a voice—until it contradicts mine.

The world revolves around me – Your dreams, emotions, and boundaries are secondary to my needs. If you expect empathy, you'll get indifference. If you seek support, you'll find criticism. I expect admiration, attention, and praise at all times, even when I give you nothing in return.

I don't like to be number 2 – I must be the best, the brightest, the most admired. If you outshine me, I'll belittle you, compete with you, or subtly sabotage your success. I see others' accomplishments not as inspiration but as threats.

If I'm not happy, nobody is going to be happy – Your peace irritates me if it exists without my permission. If I'm in a bad mood, I'll start a fight, pick at your insecurities, or create tension just to feel in control. Misery is contagious—and I intend to spread it.

If you are happy, I'll soon change that – Your happiness, if it doesn't originate from me or revolve around me, is dangerous. I'll mock it, minimize it, or manipulate you until that joy fades and I'm once again the center of your emotional universe.

We'll do it my way – Even if my way is chaos, dysfunction, or destruction, it must be followed. I value control over peace and dominance over harmony. I'd rather see you broken and obedient than strong and independent.

Your needs are negotiable—mine are non-negotiable – You're expected to give endlessly, love unconditionally, and stay loyal eternally, even when I give nothing in return. My feelings are sacred; yours are disposable.

If you try to set boundaries, I'll test, break, or punish them – Your resistance is seen as betrayal. Your attempt to protect your space will be twisted into selfishness or rejection. Boundaries threaten my power so I'll trample them with charm, rage, or guilt.

If you ever leave me, I'll either destroy your reputation or pretend you never mattered – You're either my possession or my enemy. If you walk away, I'll rewrite the story to make you the toxic one. And if I can't control you, I'll make sure no one else admires you either.

Love, to me, is control disguised as affection – I'll shower you with charm when I want something, then turn cold when you need me most. I confuse attention with love, manipulation with care, and domination with intimacy.

Remember: it's not about connection, it's about control – And as long as you stay under my spell, I'll keep rewriting the rules until there's nothing left of you that doesn't serve me.

"Smooth words may hide a wicked heart, just as a pretty glaze covers a clay pot. People may cover their hatred with pleasant words, but they're deceiving you. They pretend to be kind, but don't believe them. Their hearts are full of many evils." (Proverbs 26: 23-25 NLT)

Beneath the narcissist surface:

What people see:

- Charming
- Confidence
- Extroverts
- Sociable
- Caring

What people don't see:

- Jealous
- Bullies
- Pathological liars
- Afraid of loneliness
- Heart breakers
- No empathy
- Addicted to social attractions
- No quality of friends

Some of the *verbal* methods of a narcissist are:

- Scheming a plot of deception, distorting reality, telling half-truths, misrepresentation.
- "If you don't meet my expectations, you are guilty of neglect."
- Some play the "should" game with you: you *should* respect me, you *should* make me happy. If you don't meet these expectations, they make you feel guilty.
- The yelling tactic: yell to apply pressure, yell to unnerve, yell to intimidate.
- "If you aren't what I want you to be, I will use words to wound you."
- "You ought to meet my every need and if you don't, I'll make you feel guilty."
- "You should take care of my heart and if you don't, you are cruel."

Some of the *non-verbal* methods are:

- "My wants and wishes supersede those of everyone else."
- The silent treatment: "If you don't do what I want, you don't get my approval, my communication, or me."
- The slamming tactics: "If you don't meet my expectation, you don't deserve any dialogue with me, but I'll make my point in other ways." (i.e., slamming drawers, doors, phones, books, etc.)
- Sneering: curl the lip, roll the eyes, raise the eyebrows, etc.
- Spiteful sounds: sighs, grunts, groans, and smacking of their lips.
- Stalling tactics: slow, late, not hearing, or forgetful. "If you don't give me control, I'll take control in other ways."

People with narcissistic disorder have trouble handling anything they view as criticism. They can:

- Have major problems interacting with others and easily feel slighted
- React with rage or contempt and try to belittle other people to make themselves appear superior
- Have difficulty managing their emotions and behavior
- Experience major problems dealing with stress and adapting to change
- Withdraw from or avoid situations in which they might fail
- Feel depressed and moody because they fall short of perfection
- Have secret feelings of insecurity, shame, humiliation, and fear of being exposed as a failure

Signs you are in a narcissistic relationship:

- **You don't feel connected** – your partner talks to you only when it is convenient. They brag about themselves and their accomplishments.
- **You feel manipulated** – sometimes it's just easier to go with the flow and don't disagree. This is a way of controlling you to get what they want.
- **You don't feel good enough** – your partner puts you down or makes negative comments about the things that you do.
- **You're constantly being gaslighted** – they will gaslight you into believing some things never happened. They'll say you're not remembering correctly. Your partner will tell lies about your behavior and twist reality.
- **You avoid conversations** – a narcissist constantly tries to push your buttons to get you to react. It becomes easier to avoid having a conversation than to deal with the constant mind games.
- **You feel responsible for everything** – narcissists believe that everything is always someone else's fault. They never take responsibility for their actions and always blame someone else. Everything bad that has happened in their life is because of you.
- **You're walking on eggshells** – everything may seem fine, but then something minor happens and they go into a rage. You lose yourself because now all your decisions are based on what will keep your narcissist happy.

- **You see through the charm** – they say all the right things and make people love them because they are so nice and easy going, but the second that you're alone everything changes.
- **You feel criticized constantly** – your partner is excessively critical of your appearance; they make fun of you and put you down.
- **Your needs are ignored** – they think about their own needs and how things affect them. They will only do things that benefit themselves—not you, not the kids, and not the family as a whole.
- **Your family warns you** – sometimes your family will step forward and tell you they don't like how your partner is treating you. It becomes a point of contention with your family relationships.
- **You've been cheated on** – you may find yourself constantly questioning if your partner is being faithful because of their flirting. They might have cheated multiple times so nothing will stop them from doing it again. They love the attention a new relationship gives them.
- **You feel unloved** – you feel devalued or ignored. This is a red flag that they're not who they made themselves out to be in the first place.
- **You get the silent treatment** – your partner uses the silent treatment as a power play to control you. The silent treatment isn't part of a healthy, loving, and respectful relationship.
- **You're stuck financially** – you might be paying for everything while your partner can't hold down a job, or their job might be bringing in a lot of income but they're not

letting you see any of it. Sometimes they will hide income to make you feel trapped in the relationship.

- **You can't rely on your partner** – when they make promises, you never know if they're going to keep them. Narcissists are notorious for making promises and then breaking them when it's convenient.
- **You've asked but they won't change** – narcissists aren't willing to make changes because this would mean admitting something might be wrong within them. Remember they can do no wrong!!
- **You're the brunt of their impatience or anger** – narcissists react this way when they don't receive special recognition or treatment.

"Stay away from people who expect you to prioritize them but don't think twice about putting you last." ~ Anonymous

Reasons why you feel lonely with a narcissist:

- The relationship can't be anything but superficial
- You can't discuss anything in a civil manner
- Gaslighting and rage can exhaust you emotionally
- You are dealing with a professional faker, so you don't know where you stand

A narcissist is a con artist; they sell you a dream and deliver a living nightmare. A man will never grow up if the people around him justify his messed-up behavior.

Narcissists always target people who are better than them. If they see someone who is kind, caring, and authentic, it hurts their ego. They try to ruin their victim's life and bring them down to feed their insecurity.

A narcissist will never be grateful for what you do. They believe they're entitled to everything. The more you give, the more they take, and it will never feel like enough to them. Recognize this and stop pouring into someone who can't appreciate your worth.

It's hard to hear, but words that don't match actions are called manipulation. And refusing to be held accountable for it is called gaslighting. And once you realize this, you can see that the hardest part of getting past a narcissist is realizing you were never anything special to them. You were always just a supply. You were someone who was a place holder, someone to kill time with. But you know what's even harder to accept? They don't feel badly. They don't think they did anything wrong. They feel absolutely NOTHING!

A narcissist will provoke you to get a reaction out of you to blame everything on you. A real man doesn't play mind games with a woman. Only weak, insecure, immature boys do that. Narcissists are compulsive liars. They lie about almost everything. It gives them a feeling of superiority. They think people are too stupid to catch them. The more outrageous the lie, the more fuel they get from it.

A narcissist calls you crazy, insecure, jealous, and sensitive to keep you from the reality of:

- I lied to you
- I cheated on you
- I disrespected you

- I abandoned you
- I twisted every argument
- I made you doubt yourself
- I isolated you
- I stole everything from you

A narcissist will violate your privacy and break your trust in the worst ways. They will push you to your limits and have you questioning your own sanity. Then they'll tell people you are intentional with your reactions and that you are the problem.

Narcissists will attack the things that matter most to you. It is intentional, as they know these are the things you will most passionately defend. Often the narcissist not only doesn't want to cooperate with you and problem solve, but they also actually want to maintain the current problems and create new ones.

"Some people are upset with you because you're not suffering the way they thought you would be. Please continue to disappoint them. A narcissist will provoke you to get a reaction out of you so that they can blame it all on you." ~ Poka David

When you are in a relationship with a narcissist you will go from being the perfect love of their life to nothing you do is ever good enough. You will give everything and they will take it all and give you less and less in return. You will end up being depleted emotionally, mentally, spiritually, and probably financially too.

And then you'll get blamed for it.

Narcissists are unhappy with themselves, but their disorder tells them that all their unhappiness is caused by everyone around them. They use their unhappiness to justify their abusive, dishonest, disloyal behavior. They constantly change their minds about what they want and will always find a way to justify their wants by blaming the people who love them the most.

When you no longer let the narcissist manipulate you, be prepared to see a version of them you've never seen before. Don't let anybody make you feel crazy because you figured them out. Your safety should be a priority and if you have children, be sure to keep them safe!

A narcissist paints a picture of themselves as being the victim or innocent in all aspects. Narcissists often accuse you of doing what they are guilty of. They gaslight you to make you feel like you're the one at fault. They will be offended by the truth. But what is done in the dark will come to light. Time has a way of showing people's true colors.

Narcissists manipulate and deceive you by wearing a mask that makes them seem kind and thoughtful, hiding who they really are. Sometimes the narcissist waits until they feel like they have you before they let their mask slip. Narcissists are miserable on their own, yet they convince themselves that their misery is caused by others.

A narcissist expects you to put up with the very behaviors they're offended by because it allows them to project their own flaws onto you, essentially creating a double standard where they can criticize you for doing the same things they themselves engage in, all the while not taking responsibility for their own actions.

Narcissistic behaviors will never make sense to a rational person because the behaviors aren't based on reason. Narcissists' behaviors are based on entitlement, superiority, control, and power. They lied, cheated, gaslighted, manipulated, blame shifted, destroyed and discarded you, but somehow they're the victim...

Narcissists use mistreatment as a means to break your spirit and make you feel unimportant. They condition you to revolve the relationship around them, their wants, their needs, and their life. No matter how much you beg a narcissist to stop, they will push you past your limits until you snap. Then when you do, they'll stand back and act shocked, play the victim, and claim you're crazy.

The narcissist has trained the entire family, by example, how to treat you. Once you have been labelled as the bad one, you are fair game for siblings, spouses, children, relatives, even family friends to pick on.

All narcissists are hypocrites. They pretend to have morals and values that they really don't keep. Behind closed doors, they lie, insult, criticize, disrespect, and abuse. They can do and say whatever they want, but how dare you say anything back to them or criticize them. They have a whole set of rules but follow none of them and practice nothing of what they preach.

One person's toxic narcissist ex is now another person's toxic narcissist. They will never change. It is better to have loved and lost than to be stuck in a relationship with a narcissistic psychopath for the rest of your life. Even though I don't promote divorce, I also don't promote abuse. For your safety and your children's safety, there are times you just have to leave before you become a statistic.

Narcissistic personalities are created and sustained. No one is born a narcissist. It is a habitual choice to be selfish and to lack empathy for other people. Never forget that it is a choice. Narcissistic people don't want unconditional love. They want unconditional tolerance.

The phrase "I never feel like I am enough" is the repetition of the person in a narcissistic relationship. That's because to your narcissistic partner, you are not. No one is. Nothing is. Some people ruin the sweetest people and then call them crazy and toxic when they finally react to their disrespect.

Let's be honest—someone who destroys your mental health cannot be the love of your life. Stay away from people who act like a victim in a problem they created. Narcissists need the approval reinforcement of others to distract themselves from their feelings of worthlessness.

Everyone should accept accountability. I owe myself an apology for letting others be comfortable with treating me like I'm nothing. Nobody is perfect but there is no way you're going to convince me that my reaction to your actions is the problem.

When a narcissist doesn't treat others in the same way, it's all the proof you need. They know it's wrong, their treatment of you is intentional, and they're fully capable of behaving better. They're just choosing not to.

Narcissists learn what you value and love deeply, and in doing so, they know what to attack for control and punishment. However, it's a small sacrifice to accept the narcissist's false portrayal of you when you escape their toxic presence and drama. Don't engage with them. Let them spread their tales; your life will bloom. Their deceit and bitterness will poison their own existence. They will reap the disaster of their lies eventually.

The narcissist doesn't want your love because they don't know what love is. They want your admiration and your obedience as a player in their fake make-believe world. If they are more focused on how you react instead of how they treat you or what they did to cause your reaction, that is manipulation!

Narcissists rewrite history to escape accountability. You are not crazy! Remember this...selfish people don't care about you unless you are doing something for them. Let me say it again; words not matching actions is called manipulation, and when a narcissist refuses to be held accountable for their words, it is called gaslighting.

The reason you can never win against a narcissist isn't because you aren't as smart as they are. It's because your conscience will never allow you to sink to their level. A narcissist would rather impress a stranger than care for their own family.

"A narcissist will change you. They will steal your innocence. They will steal your joy. They will break your spirit until there's nothing left, and then they will blame you. Accusing you of ruining things."
~ Maria Consiglio

The narcissist will deliberately distort your reality and make you question your own memory, perception, and sanity. Your entire relationship with a narcissist is based on deception. You are lied to and deceived from the beginning. A narcissist doesn't break your heart—they break your spirit. That's why it takes so long to heal.

A narcissist will manipulate everyone around you to betray you. This is not a reflection of who you are but more of a reflection of the narcissist's powers of manipulation and the integrity of other people.

Narcissists often stop their abuse with sporadic periods of seeming kindness and warmth. This causes you to become trauma-bonded to them, constantly trying to make them happy. What is trauma-bonded you may ask! Trauma-bonding is a deep, unhealthy emotional attachment a victim forms with their abuser. Then, when they again turn abusive, you may believe you deserve it.

The narcissist drowns in their own jealousy. The narcissist is jealous of anyone they view as having more than them. If you are confident, happy, well-liked, successful, or simply fulfilled in life, the narcissist will not be able to stand it. Even though the narcissist does not like you, they do not want anyone else to have you and treat you well. The jealousy is extreme when you succeed without them.

A narcissist's reaction to this overwhelming jealousy that is directed at you is full of contradictions and denial. Their thinking goes somewhat like this:

- That didn't happen, and if it did, it wasn't that bad...
- And if it was, it's not a big deal...
- And if it is, I didn't mean to do it...
- And if I did do it, then it was your fault.

They are more focused on how you react instead of how they treat you or what they do to cause your pain. The narcissist remembers everything; the only problem is those things never happened the way they remember them.

A narcissist will not change; they just blame everything on everybody else and then move on to someone unaware of their manipulation. Narcissists don't change because they don't want to change. They want to keep on using and abusing because it gets them the attention they so desperately crave.

Narcissists paint a picture of themselves as being victims or innocent in all aspects. They will be offended by the truth. But what is done in the dark will come to light. Time has a way of showing people's true colors. Narcissists' behaviors will never make sense to a rational person because their behaviors aren't based in reason. Narcissists' behaviors are based on entitlement, superiority, control, and power.

Narcissists don't act abusive in front of everyone. They act caring, loving, and respectful in front of others they want to impress or want to be well regarded by. They not only want the accolades and praise for their behaviors, they want to make sure that when you start opening up about their real actions, whether verbal or physical, no one will believe you.

Narcissists are great actors and carefully select their audience.

When you marry a narcissistic man, you never get the chance to be a wife. Instead, you take on the role of a mother because these grown adults behave like man-children. They go to work Monday through Friday and then spend their weekends sitting in front of a laptop, downloading music, playing video games (or any of their other hobbies), or creating messes for you to clean. You find yourself both single and a parent simultaneously, shouldering the weight of responsibilities without the support of a partner.

Suffering In Silence

Narcissists don't marry for love or partnership; they marry because they want a maid, cook, secretary, banker, caretaker, sex slave, and a babysitter. They crave control, not connection. Their selfish desires consume them, leaving you to manage the household, raise the children, and cater to their every whim. Your dreams of a loving, equal relationship are shattered, replaced by the harsh reality of slavery.

As the days turn into weeks, and the weeks into years, you become a shadow of your former self. Your identity is erased, replaced by the exhausting duties of managing a narcissist's life. You're forced to sacrifice your own desires, interests, and friendships to accommodate their demands. The emotional labor is suffocating, leaving you drained, resentful, and wondering how you ended up in this nightmare.

You're not alone in this struggle. Many women have fallen prey to the charming facade of a narcissist only to find themselves trapped in a loveless, thankless role. Remember, you deserve better. You deserve a partner who loves, supports, and respects you. Don't let the narcissist's gaslighting convince you otherwise.

Break free from this toxic cycle and reclaim your life. You are more than a mother to a man-child; you are a strong, capable, and worthy individual who deserves to be loved and cherished. Remember this is a form of abusive behavior! Toxicity is when they can't let you go but they can't treat you right either!

Narcissists drive you to insanity with their criticisms, rudeness, accusations, cruelty, condemning sense of superiority, riding their moral high horse, projection, hypocrisy, deaf ears, control, lies, threats, and double standards. Then when you react, they say you are overly dramatic and you are the one in need of help. They are the most immature blame shifters you will ever know, full of nothing but excuses and justification for their pathetic behaviors.

A narcissist will flaunt deliberately giving to another person what you've asked—not because they value the other person, but because they are obsessed and fixated with pulling you down. Their behavior is cruel in so many ways.

No one can throw bigger tantrums than a narcissist who's losing control of someone's mind. The reason they don't see a problem with their actions isn't just because of their own arrogance, but because they surround themselves with people who normalize it.

A narcissist's idea of peace is that you should absorb all their toxicity in silence and never complain. And to top it off? When the world watches, you better play the role of the perfect happy wife.

Sometimes we have to remind ourselves that we are not responsible for other people's poor behavior towards us, or their gaslighting, or their manipulation, or their unkindness. That's on them. What's on you is how you choose to respond, set boundaries, know your worth, and not let their actions impact the beautiful soul that you are.

The narcissist wants you to believe there is something you could have done to change the outcome of the relationship. This is a lie! You are not toxic! Many times, we are pushed to become a person we don't want to be due to the treatment we have endured. Once we respond in a negative, defensive manner, the narcissist project that we are crazy!

"Narcissists never enter a conversation; they enter into verbal competitions. Their goal is to win at all costs! They have no interest in seeking understanding, clarification, compromise, or reaching

a meeting of the minds. Their conversations are only meant to manipulate, confuse, control, destabilize, deflect accountability, cast doubt, distort reality, and create drama." ~ Narcissistic Families Inc.

When being abused, leave. Not for ego but for self-respect and safety. Leaving a relationship with a narcissist is like peeling back the layers of an onion. Little by little you realize all the different ways you have been abused. More and more things start to unfold, and you see more clearly the many ways they manipulated and took advantage of you. As time goes on, you realize the abuse was so much worse than you even thought. Once you can distance yourself from the abuse, you gain a much clearer picture.

A narcissist often doesn't take responsibility for their actions. If you confront them about something they've done to you, they're likely to hold a grudge. Instead of admitting their mistakes, they might get upset with you for pointing those mistakes out and may not forgive you for it. This is because they typically have a hard time accepting that they could be at fault.

Do not tell a narcissist that they have hurt your feelings. They don't have empathy. They won't feel badly about how they made you feel. They will take it as criticism and get angry. It will backfire. And do not shed tears—they see that as a sign of weakness and will only disrespect you more. Most domestic violence calls that often end up with a death are the result of the violence perpetrated by a narcissist person.

You can't fix a toxic/abusive/narcissistic person. You can't change them. You can't get them to look at themselves, have self-respect, understand, or gain self-awareness. They rarely learn healthier communication skills because they are emotionally immature. Their ego won't allow them to admit to any wrongdoing or make sincere apologies. They rarely seek help, unless it's to continue to manipulate. You can't teach them compassion. You can't force them to be respectful, because feeling entitled and being disrespectful is part of their character and who they are. You can't make them listen, because they just don't give a darn. The only thing you can do is heal yourself. Empower yourself with knowledge on abuse, use boundaries, and cut complete contact.

"Narcissists will stand there and watch you cry over the pain they have caused with a glint in their eye, a smirk on their face, no remorse, no apology, and they will keep winding you up and blaming you for the pain they're causing you." ~ Anonymous

When a malignant narcissist attempts to insult you, in reality it's a compliment even though it wasn't intended that way from their end. Why? Because what they are really saying is: "You threaten me. Your light shines too brightly, that's why I have to dim it. You have too much support in your corner, that's why I have to try to alienate and isolate you. You are too visible in your gifts and assets, that's why I have to shame you into hiding yourself. Your inner and outer beauty is too apparent, that's why I have to make you doubt yourself. Your intelligence, intuition, and discernment are razor sharp, that's why I have to gaslight you into disbelieving it. Your voice is too powerful, that's why I have to silence it."

"Narcissists don't want honest relationships, they want cheerleaders. They want people who always give them the right. They want blind loyalty. They want unconditional acceptance, no matter what they do. As long as you don't question anything they do, or give them the

wrong on anything, they might just leave you alone. But watch out if you disagree with them or go against them in any way. And it never goes unpunished. Narcissists are spiteful and vindictive."
~ Maria Consiglio

Do narcissists follow the same pattern in every relationship? Absolutely! They have the same exact pattern in all their physical relationships. They get excited to be with someone new and express it. They show every positive trait and dedicate their full attention to the person. Then the excitement starts to wear off and their negative behaviors start to show. Love bombing is followed by reality and that's when the arguments begin.

Narcissists love it when their target sits quietly and tolerates their disrespect, verbal attacks, rudeness, cruelty, bullying, arrogance, control, and manipulation. But they despise the ones who defend themselves, stand up to them, speak up, expose them, disagree with them, see their double standards, and those who won't comply with their demands, orders, expectations, threats, or other controlling and bullying behaviors. They hold hate and contempt when they can't take someone's power away.

Once you know you are dealing with a narcissist, you have to completely drop any expectations you would have in normal human interactions. This person is not going to get it.

One unpleasant but crucial part of the healing process from narcissistic abuse is accepting that you weren't even in a relationship. You were in a MANIPULATIONSHIP with an immoral and very sick pathological liar who would (and probably did behind your back) have sex with anyone (or anything) who gave him or her any attention.

A narcissist rewrites history to escape accountability. Narcissists are unhappy with themselves, but their disorder tells them that all their unhappiness is caused by everyone around them. They use their unhappiness to justify their abusive, dishonest, and disloyal behavior. They constantly change their minds about what they want and will always find a way to justify their wants by blaming the people who love them the most for not providing them with those wants. A narcissist thinks: "How dare you ruin my reputation by telling the truth about what I said and did."

Narcissists enjoy manipulating other people's emotions, which is why you should never take anything they say to you personally. They are provoking you to get a reaction, to cause drama, and to stir up negative emotions. Belittling, criticizing, and judging others makes them feel superior. Emotional manipulation is when you deliberately hurt someone and expect them to forgive you and move on.

Narcissists often have secret lives. They lie with ease. They can cheat without remorse. They are two faced, often appearing to have an impeccable and perfect public image that most people will buy into. Behind closed doors, where nobody on the outside can see, they will inflict tremendous damage to family members, often including their own children. Their lack of empathy can be deceptive.

If you marry a narcissist, you won't get to be a real spouse. You end up doing everything alone like a single parent, but without the freedom of being single. Narcissists don't marry for love; they want someone to care for them and follow their rules. They don't want a real relationship; they want control. You'll be the one managing the house, raising the kids, and making sure everything runs smoothly while they focus only on themselves. The dream of a happy, equal marriage disappears, and you'll be left feeling like a servant.

Remember, you deserve a partner who truly loves and respects you. Don't let a narcissist make you believe otherwise. You are strong, valuable, and worthy of real love. It's never too late to break free and take back your life.

People who are guilty of mistreating you are offended by everything. You can't change someone who doesn't see an issue with their actions. Don't let anybody make you second guess yourself when you begin figuring them out.

You can defeat a narcissist (even though you can't change them) without saying a single word. Just do these seven things:

1. **Stay unpredictable.**
   Narcissists crave control. When you act in ways they can't anticipate, they lose their grip on you.
2. **Control your emotions.**
   They use your feelings against you. When you stop reacting and stay calm, you take away their power.
3. **Believe their behavior, not their words.**
   Don't fall for what they say, watch what they do. Their charm is just a mask; pay attention to their true actions.
4. **Focus on your growth.**
   Succeed in ways they never thought you could. Improve your health, finances, and goals—not to prove a point to them, but to elevate yourself beyond their reach.

5. **Let go emotionally.**
   Total detachment hurts them more than anything. When you no longer care, they lose the ability to affect you.
6. **Cut the energy cords.**
   They drain your spirit. Stop replaying the past or holding onto the good moments. Protect your peace and release their hold on your energy.
7. **Don't let their voice live in your mind.**

That critical inner voice? It's not yours, it's theirs. Talk back to it, shut it down, and don't let shame or fear control your life. You're free now.

**Do you feel emotionally drained
or like you are walking on eggshells?**

**Do you feel safe and comfortable being yourself
around this person?**

**Do they respect your boundaries
or do they try to violate them?**

4
Cheater, Cheater: Trust and Lies

"The trust of the innocent is the liar's most useful tool."
~ Stephen King

The lies they tell about you will never change the truth about them! Everyone wants the truth, but no one wants to be honest. No one is more hated than those who tell the truth. No one is more committed to trashing your name than the person who is worried about you telling the truth. One lie can end a million trusts.

Who else feels like we're getting too old to be around people who don't understand the concept of loyalty and honesty? They both seem like a rare commodity these days. It has become very hard to find the truth in all and every situation. Truth does not mind being questioned. However, a lie does not like being challenged.

"The truth always comes out in the end, no matter how hard anyone tries to hide it or stop it. Lies are just a temporary delay to the inevitable." ~ Author Unknown

For my part, I only trust ACTIONS! I don't trust words anymore. People can tell you anything, but actions tell you everything. PEOPLE lie...actions don't. They lie because what they want is more important to them than your respect. They are willing to sacrifice your trust for whatever it is they desire. A single lie discovered is enough to create doubt in every truth expressed. A liar will get mad at you for knowing the truth. As has been said, truth does not mind being questioned; a lie does not like being challenged. The only people who get mad at you for speaking the truth are those people who are living a lie. KEEP speaking the truth. You have to answer for your actions, not theirs.

Anything you lose by speaking your truth isn't a loss; it's an alignment. The only people who are mad at you for speaking the truth are those people who are living a lie. Keep speaking the truth! The only thing more shocking than the truth are the things people do to cover it up. A real man will be honest, no matter how painful the truth is. A COWARD hides behind lies and deceit. It's wild how a woman's intuition can feel the betrayal long before the truth ever shows itself.

"A person who can consciously hurt you, lie about you, try to destroy your credibility knowing very well that you are trustworthy, is a person with no conscience. And a person with no conscience is a very dangerous person." ~ Steven Ingram, The Bat Wolf

The reason people make up false stories about you is because they don't like the fact that they can no longer control you, so they recruit everyone else to hate you to make themselves feel powerful. People will lie directly to your face and then get mad at you because you don't trust them. When toxic people know they've done you wrong, they'll often become fixated on trying to destroy your reputation by spreading lies and misleading information.

"However no matter how much you deny the truth, the truth goes on existing." ~ George Orwell

Accountability is so important throughout your entire life. Nobody is perfect, but there is no way you should be convinced that your reaction to their actions is the problem. A man who can't answer your questions without getting angry or defensive is hiding more than the answer, remember that! Loyalty is not tested when things are easy; it's tested during hard times.

There are people who have to see you as the problem. They do this because if you're the problem, it means they are not. And if they're not the problem, then they never have to change or disrupt anything. You are the only keeper of your happiness. Stop giving people the power to control your smile, your worth, and your attitude.

"God didn't remove the Red Sea...he parted it. He isn't going to remove the situation, but He will make a way through it. Trust that God is always on time. Even when we think He is too late."
~ Barbra Svosvera

"I know it's a hard lesson to learn, but the truth is you cannot love yourself and love someone who hurts you at the same time. Please choose you." ~ Stephanie Bennett-Henry

You don't have to cheat to lose someone. You can lose someone from a lack of communication, attention, and disrespect. It's not always what you do; sometimes it's about what you didn't do. Talking to the opposite sex behind your spouse's back is still cheating, by the way.

Never ignore a person who cares for you, because someday you'll realize you've lost a diamond while you were busy collecting stones. And stones have far less value than the diamond you lost!

Suffering In Silence

You can't change people, so don't drive yourself crazy trying. Instead, just change how you deal with them or just stay away from them. Whoever betrays you once will betray you a thousand times. As an unknown author stated, you don't have to drink the whole sea to realize that it's salty. It's better to have nobody than to have someone who is half there or doesn't want to be there.

"Better to be slapped with the truth than kissed with a lie."
~ Author Unknown

If you tell the truth, it becomes a part of your past. But if you lie, it becomes a part of your future. Never lie to a woman because she's going to find out anyway. Most women investigate better than the FBI! When lies bring people together, the truth will eventually tear them apart. Stay true to yourself; integrity always wins at the end. The most genuine people will tell you the truth even if it makes them look bad because they value integrity over being liked by everyone. When your intentions are pure, you don't lose anyone, they lose you.

"Whoever abandons you in the middle of the ocean has
no right to know what the sharks did to you and how you
managed it to the shore." ~ Author Unknown

Don't worry about the haters. They are just angry because the truth you speak contradicts the lie they live. When you stand up and speak the truth, you don't just make noise, you make enemies. Truth disrupts comfort.

If you want to be trusted later, you must be honest now. When someone lies to you, it's because they don't respect you enough to be honest, and they think you are too stupid to know the difference. An old saying states that lies have short legs, and truth has long arms. Secrets and lies kill relationships. No matter how careful you are, you will get caught. What's done in darkness always comes to light.

Don't lie to an over thinker because it never ends well. Such people have trained their brains to look for holes in a story. If things don't make sense, they will think about it over and over until it makes sense.

"I may not wake up with a man beside me, but I wake up with coffee and coffee doesn't hide a cell phone and lie about talking to other women." ~ Author Unknown

Do you often end up doing what they want you to do, rather than what you want?

You shall not commit adultery. (Deuteronomy 5:18 NASB)

But a man who commits adultery has no sense; whoever does so destroys himself. (Proverbs 6:32 NIV)

But I tell you that anyone who looks at a woman lustfully has already committed adultery with her in his heart. (Matthew 5:28 NIV)

Do nothing out of selfish ambitions or vain conceit. Rather, in humility value others above yourselves. (Philippians 2:3 NIV)

Relationships

"Don't let the ugly in others kill the beauty in you!"
~ Author Unknown

Without Communication there is no Relationship

Without Respect there is no Love

Without Trust there is no reason to Continue

The same people who derisively say "you've changed" tend to forget they never grew. Some will see your flame and want to blow it out; others will approach it with a candle. And just because someone is "family" doesn't mean you have to tolerate lies, chaos, drama, manipulation, and disrespect. Often the people who hurt you most are those you are the closest to. People can't do ugly things to other people and expect to live a beautiful life. It just doesn't work that way!

"Saying sorry is not an apology; saying sorry is simply an acknowledgement of what you did. The actual apology comes from showing through future actions and behaviors that when you said you were sorry you actually meant it, because sorry means nothing if nothing changes." ~ Mark Smith

Cheating in a relationship often happens when one of the partners start paying more attention to what they think they're missing instead of being grateful for what they already have. Being sneaky behind the back of a good person will always catch up to you. In Matthew 19:9 Jesus addresses that sexual immorality is biblical grounds for divorce

(which includes adultery, incest, homosexuality, prostitution, and pornography.)

If you can cheat on your spouse and come home, look them in the eye and tell them you love them, then you're the lowest kind of person on the pyramid. Cheating is a personal decision. Some people will never cheat no matter how hard things are; others will always cheat no matter how good they have it. If you make the decision to cheat, that is no one else's fault except for your own, so don't try to lie to and blame everyone else. Cheating may start out as a thrill but be prepared for the end results when the cheating comes to the surface. Is what you have worth losing for what you MIGHT gain?

A man who loves you does not have wandering eyes for other women. A man that runs to another woman when his home is having problems is a WEAK MAN. Keep the man who respects you and your boundaries, not the one who lusts after others. A mistake is an accident. Cheating and lying are not mistakes—they are intentional choices. It is a decision to break your partner's trust, hurt their feelings, and destroy their life along with your family just to satisfy selfish needs.

Beyond sexual immorality and abandonment, other scenarios may justify a biblically permissible divorce. These include:

1. **Physical Abuse:** Persistent physical abuse violates the marriage vow to love and cherish and poses a threat to the spouse's well-being.
2. **Verbal and Emotional Abuse:** Continuous verbal cruelty and emotional manipulation can be equally destructive.

3. **Addictions:** Unrepentant addictions to drugs, alcohol, or gambling is a threat to the family's welfare.
4. **Sexual Immorality:** Persistent engagement in pornography or other sexual sins violates the marriage covenant.
5. **Threats of Harm:** Verbal threats of physical harm or actual physical violence takes away from the inherent worth of the victim.

We end up in toxic relationships because we don't stand up for ourselves early on when red flags occur. We let behaviors slide because we fear losing a companion. How long do you let disrespect and neglect go? At some point, you have to develop healthy barriers for how you're going to be treated. You're responsible for your involvement, nobody else is. Never date a man who has abandoned his kids or doesn't support them. Any man who isn't loyal to his children will never be loyal to anyone.

The way a man fits you into his schedule says a lot about how he thinks of you. Never beg for love, attention, or respect. If it's not freely given, it's not worth having. Don't let anyone save you for later. Masculinity isn't toxic, the absence of it is. Weak men are abusive and spiteful; strong masculine men are protective and loving.

Real love is not based on romance, candlelight dinners, and walks along the beach. It is based on respect, compromise, care, and trust. A good loyal woman is one of the greatest things a man can have in his life. But it takes a real man to realize that. A woman doesn't walk away from a man because he made a mistake. She walks away from her man because he made those mistakes a habit.

A stay-at-home mom should never have to prove her worth. Just because she doesn't bring in a check doesn't mean she has no value. She's doing important things too. She is amazing and she's worth so, so much more than a paycheck. The statistics of the worth of a stay-at-home mom is mind blowing when you see the facts and figures. Today's calculations of a stay-at-home mom is worth $184,000 annually. That's right—annually! Who contributes to the family?

Women, you are not a rehabilitation center for badly raised men. It is not your job to fix him, change him, parent him, or raise him. You want a partner, not a project. Graveyards are full of women who were told, "Hang in there. He'll change."

At Charlie Kirk's memorial, his wife Erika Kirk challenged men and women to build stronger relationships. She stated, "To all the men watching around the world, accept Charlie's challenge and embrace true manhood. Be strong and courageous for your families. Love your wives and lead them. Love your children and protect them. Be the spiritual head of your home. But please be a leader worth following. Your wife is not your servant. Your wife is not your employee. Your wife is not your slave. She is your helper. You are not rivals. You are one flesh working together for the glory of God. Women, I have a challenge for you too. Be virtuous. Our strength is found in God's design for our role. We are the guardians. We are the encouragers. We are the preservers. Guard your heart. Everything you do flows from it. And if you're a mother, please recognize that is the single most important ministry you have."

Beyond a marital standpoint, there is evidence strong relationships contribute to a long, healthy, and happy life. People with strong social relationships are 50 percent less likely to die prematurely. Having a caring friend can provide a buffer against the effects of stress. A 2012 International Gallup poll found that people who feel they have friends and families to count on are generally more satisfied with their personal health than people who feel isolated.

Building Strong Relationships

- **Powerful listening** goes beyond hearing words and messages; it connects us emotionally with the one we are communicating with.
- **Empathy** is the foundation of good two-way communication.
- **Choose** emotions and words wisely.
- **Acting authentically** means acting with integrity. It means living in harmony with your values. Be yourself!
- **Look for and accentuate the positive** qualities in others. Humbly acknowledge the difference people make in your life.

4 rules needed in a relationship:

1. Communication
2. Leave the past in the past
3. Loyalty and love
4. Don't let your friends influence your decisions in the relationship.

A healthy bond grows through honest connection and mutual respect. Focus on the present, stay devoted, and protect your trust.

Keep decisions personal between the two sides, free from outside interference, for a lasting partnership.

A relationship means you come together to make each other better. Believe in each other. Support each other. Build each other. Be their peace, not their problem. A true friend is someone who knows how crazy you are and is still willing to be seen in public with you!

Dysfunctional families tend to cater to the most toxic person. The other family members do everything in their power to keep the toxic person happy. The people who know your triggers and trigger you on purpose, these people are never someone you can trust in a relationship, they're never someone who will have your best interests at heart, and any relationship with them should always be on a superficial level. Be cordial or simply ignore them at family gatherings. Don't invite them over for supper. Remember that they truly don't have your best interest in mind.

The strength of a relationship is not measured by how much you agree, but by how well you navigate your differences. No matter how educated, talented, rich, or cool you believe you are, how you treat people ultimately tells all. Integrity is everything. You can't build healthy relationships with people who dismiss your feelings or refuse to communicate. Love isn't enough when respect, consideration, and emotional safety are missing.

You are enough. Someone leaving your life doesn't change that. But it does create space for you to get what you deserve. So, heal, smile, and trust in what's to come. The other person will never know what they've lost because let's be honest, they never knew what they had.

You can't save somebody who isn't willing to participate in their own rescue. It's pointless.

"An immature man won't end a relationship directly. He'll sabotage it or push you to be the one who walks away." ~ Ismael Gomez III

A relationship with no trust is like a car with no gas. You can stay in it, but it won't go anywhere. Never feel guilty for moving on from someone who had every opportunity to treat you properly but never thought it was worth doing. However, every marriage is worth fighting to save but not all marriages can be saved if both parties are not willing to participate.

The worst feeling for a woman is when she tries to have a conversation with a man about his behavior that hurts her every day, but instead of listening, he gets angry and turns the situation around on her. When a woman moves on, it is not because she doesn't want to work it out. No, it is because she is exhausted from being in a one-sided relationship. She is exhausted from being lied to, from being taken advantage of. When a woman leaves, it is not because she wants to but because she has to!

In a toxic relationship, it's easy for outsiders to look at a woman and think she's blind, naïve, or stupid for staying...but what they don't realize is, she knows. She knows exactly what's going on. She sees the lies, feels the disrespect, and recognizes the patterns. She's not clueless, she's calculating. She's preparing. She is living it!

If a man loves you, he will never fill your ears with lies, your mouth with words, your eyes with tears, your mind with confusion, or your heart with pain. If a man expects a woman to be an angel in his life, he must first create heaven for her. Angels don't live in hell. And when you get to the point where you have to remove someone from your life, they will never tell people the full story. They will only tell them the part that makes you look bad and them in the best light. And that's okay. The truth will eventually surface. Safety is more important than what people think of you and your decisions.

Stop sending long paragraphs and messages explaining how you feel. Just don't say anything. Often it doesn't matter what you say. If they don't care, they just don't. And nothing you say will change that. Keep your guard up.

I have three rules:

1. Don't lie to me
2. Don't use me
3. If you're tired of me, leave me alone

Your Children:

Kids do not need a perfect home; they just need a safe one! A place where they feel loved, understood, and supported. A place where they feel comfortable knowing they belong. A peaceful place to live.

When you choose to be a parent, you accept the fact that you'll be worried about the safety of your kids for the rest of your life. You are not just raising your kids, you're raising someone's future wife, mom, husband, father, friend, etc. Raise them with intention. Raise your kids to be GOOD people. No matter how tired you are after work, interact with your kids because they've been waiting all day for you.

Being raised by a narcissistic father means your father hasn't fully matured emotionally. His main focus is his own needs, the way he's perceived by others, and being "respected" by his family. He tends to confuse respect with obedience. This toxic legacy fosters inner conflict, people-pleasing habits, and a deep-seated need for self-redemption and healing in their children. As a result, children of narcissistic parents often struggle with feelings of inadequacy, anxiety, and self-doubt. They may feel like they're walking on eggshells, never knowing what will trigger their parent's anger or disappointment. This can lead to a constant sense of hypervigilance, as they're always trying to anticipate and meet their parent's needs.

A child's shoulders were not meant to bear the weight of their parent's choices. Teach your kids all feelings are valid, but not all behaviors are acceptable. You don't get a second chance at raising your kids so be present and go hard for them. We all should want our children to look back and say, "My mom or dad faced every obstacle, pushed through every challenge, and still came out on top. She (or he) was unstoppable, and that means I can be too." Our mom had many challenges in her life, but she didn't face many of them. She chose to be silent and suffer alone.

As a parent, it's your job to rearrange your life to benefit your children. However, there is a difference between spoiling a child and finding a good balance for the benefit of your child. Your children come before your wants. As a parent, your role is to create a stable, safe, and loving environment for your children, even if it means making significant changes to your own life. We should be trading our WANTS for our children's NEEDS. Remember, a child doesn't always get their way. You must remain in the parent position. There is nothing more important in this world than your children, and raising good children is your responsibility as a parent.

When your children desire to talk to you and share their problems with you, stop everything and listen to them. In today's busy world, trying to make the most of your time and trying to manage your to-do list makes it very hard to stop and listen sometimes. There is nothing more important than for a parent to listen to their kids. If you don't, someone else will and who will be that someone else? You can make all the money in the world, but if you're not making memories with your kids or investing in your kids, you have still failed in life.

As a child I remember trying to talk about something that happened in school or something that we as kids were facing, and our dad would say "That is kids' nonsense. We don't need to hear about that!" The things that are important to your kids should be important to you. An adult's priorities and children's priorities are different at different points of life, but that doesn't mean it is not important to listen to them.

As a mother, your job is to protect your kids from toxic situations and people. A mother protecting her children from a toxic, inconsistent father isn't bitter—it's being a good mom and protecting your kids. Co-parenting with the same person you're trying to heal from is incredibly hard. An absent father is better than the presence of a toxic one. One thing I will never take lightly is how one makes a child feel. Nothing in this world matters more to me than their hearts. Shout out to the moms doing it all for the kids while the other parent does whatever they want. You're incredible!

Choose your kids. In every situation, at any time, over anyone, choose your kids! Many people will pass through your life for a season, but your children will always be your children. Make sure the choices you make are worth the losses you will take. Be a mother to your kids before you try to be a woman to a man.

Narcissistic parents don't want to raise children. They want to be SEEN as good parents. The camera comes out for social media but DISAPPEARS when real parenting work begins. Their public faces and private behavior tell two completely different stories.

Often times an ex will try to sabotage the kids because of how much love your kids show for you. A mother who takes on both the role of a father and a mother deserves appreciation, not criticism. She deserves to be cherished and honored for the resilience she shows every day.

A narcissistic man fails as a man and a dad when they harm the emotional stability of their children's mother, knowing she is primary source of strength and support.

How to raise mentally strong kids:

- Encourage problem solving
- Teach emotional resilience
- Praise effort, not results
- Let them fail
- Teach self-discipline
- Encourage a growth mindset
- Set healthy boundaries
- Model mental strength
- Normalize challenges
- Teach gratitude
- Encourage independence

- Teach healthy coping skills
- Encourage positive self-talk
- Help them manage anxiety
- Avoid overprotecting
- Let them make decisions
- Teach them to set goals
- Teach them delayed gratification

Someday your children are going to figure things out, I promise you. They'll learn to recognize the type of parent you are, the type of spouse you are, and how you treat other people. They'll recognize how much effort you put into them. You're either going to be someone they look up to or someone they never want to be like. Always remember they are watching and absorbing everything whether you know it or not. Kids are smart—they have eyes and ears. They hear and see everything that is happening around them!

Toxic Relationships

Remove yourself from toxic people and toxic relationships. Don't let them suck you into their poison. Relationships are about trust. If you constantly feel like you need to spy on your partner, then it's time to evaluate your current situation. Toxic is when they can't let you go but they can't treat you right either.

When you fall in love with someone, you aren't interested in anyone else. If you are, you aren't in love, and I think everyone needs to hear that. ~ Unknown Author

Most men aren't running away from a great woman. They are running away from parts of themselves they are not willing to fix to deserve her. Your partner is supposed to be your safe space, not another battle in life. Love is nothing without action, trust is nothing without proof, and apologies are nothing without change.

"Our brains are wired for connection, but trauma rewires them for protection. That's why healthy relationships are difficult for wounded people." ~ Ryan North

The man or woman you choose to be your partner affects everything in your life: your mental health, your peace of mind, the love inside of you, your happiness, how you get through tragedies, your success, how your children will be raised and so much more. Choose very wisely.

"He's broken; I think I can fix him. Sis, he's got eight other women trying to fix him—don't be part of the construction crew."
~ Author Unknown

If you need to tell them to help carry the bricks, they aren't the ones to build with. If they are not doing anything to keep you, then why are you fighting to stay?

Remember, they cheated because they wanted to, they lied because they could, and now they're sorry because they got caught. It's always about them. You did nothing to cause or deserve it. Don't ever let ANYONE make you feel crazy because you figured them out.

Some people will learn how to appreciate you by losing you. Go where you are celebrated, not tolerated. If people treat you like an option, leave them like a choice. You're worth being loved and valued. Relationships must be a two-way street to be healthy relationships.

A man should take care of his woman, and a woman should take care of her man. No one is before the other. Love is all about teamwork. Immature people who know they've done you wrong will always distance themselves to avoid accountability.

The only people who will be mad at you for telling the truth are those people that are living a lie. Keep telling the truth. Lies have become so acceptable that people get offended when you tell them the truth.

A man or woman can apologize, cry, fake illnesses, even faint, and still be lying. Do not get upset with people or situations; both are powerless without your reaction. Move on like you never knew them, because in reality? You didn't.

Most people mess up something good by looking for something better, only to end up with something worse. Sometimes the people you wanted as a part of your story are only meant to be a chapter. Sometimes you have to cut ties with people who aren't good for you. The love isn't lost, but the communication isn't healthy. Move on!

No one can mess with your spouse unless they are interested. Ever notice after a breakup the loyal one stays single and deals with the damage until healed? The cheater is already in another relationship. A real spouse chooses to honor, love, respect, adore, and be faithful to one partner.

It's really easy for an unfaithful partner to walk away because they already have their next option lined up. It's harder for the loyal partner to walk away because they weren't looking for happiness elsewhere. When a spouse replaces you with peace and not another partner, it's really over. The saddest thing about BETRAYAL is that it never comes from your ENEMIES!

If a woman is talking to your man, she's not the problem, he is. The fact that another woman feels comfortable invading space that belongs to you reflects on how your man acts behind your back. If he were a loyal man, he wouldn't give another woman the opportunity to be around. Cheaters often accuse you of cheating. Liars often accuse you of lying. Insecure people make you feel insecure. Pay attention to how people treat you. It's a reflection of who they really are.

Cheating isn't always kissing, touching, or flirting. If one is keeping secrets, deleting messages, or feeling like they have to hide things, then they are already there. A toxic person will never change. They just change victims and blame everything on everybody else.

If you want a strong relationship, don't ever give up, don't lie to your partner, and don't become a cheater. We become a reflection of how we are treated. If you don't like how someone is acting, how are you treating them?

"If another girl steals your man, there's no better revenge than letting her keep him. Real men can't be stolen." ~ Stranger Word

"I can't believe what you say, because I can see what you do."
~ James Baldwin

Never ignore a person who loves you, cares for you, and misses you. One day you might wake up and realize you lost the moon while counting the stars. People who want to see you win, will help you win. Remember that.

You can't build healthy relationships with people who dismiss your feelings or refuse to communicate. Love isn't enough when respect, consideration, and emotional safety are missing.

What other factors could this person in your relationship be dealing with right now?

How do you typically react when you feel triggered or challenged in a relationship?

Fear

"Fear is the lock; courage is the key to freedom." ~ Joseph Campbell

"F-E-A-R has two meanings: Forget Everything And Run or Face Everything And Rise. The choice is yours." ~ Zig Ziglar

"Be strong and courageous. Do not be afraid or terrified because of them, for the Lord your God goes with you; he will never leave you nor forsake you." (Deuteronomy 31:6 NIV)

Both faith and fear demand that you believe in something you can't see. You choose! Many times, our greatest fear is failure. Failure is a necessary part of life. We would be wise to allow it to change us and shape us. Don't be afraid to start over again. This time you're not starting from scratch; you're starting from experience.

However, there are different types of fear. There are rational fears, irrational fears, and primal or specific phobias. Rational fears are based on real or imminent threats. Irrational fears or phobias are intense, persistent fears of specific objects or situations that can pose a real threat. Primal fears are instinctive or built into our brains.

Replacing anxiety, fear, and sadness with humor is another excellent way to cope with real or imagined failures. In this regard, imagining your own failure can be a major cause of performance anxiety. If you can find ways to distract yourself from your fear of failure, you can actually prevent the failure from happening.

People who have strong fears about the unknown have a strong need to "know everything" beforehand. No one ever knows how to do something before they do it. You have to learn as you go.

"I am not concerned that you have fallen.
I am concerned that you arise." ~ Abraham Lincoln

Strategies to manage failure:

- **Don't make it personal** – separate the failure from your identity. Just because you haven't found a successful way of doing something doesn't mean you are failure.
- **Learn and adapt** – what did you learn from this and how will you apply what you have learned moving forward?
- **Stop dwelling on it** – obsessing over your failure will not change the outcome.
- **Release the need for approval of others** – this is your life, not theirs.

- **Try a new point of view** – steer away from the negative things

Guide to overcoming failure:

- Admit the experience
- Recognize failure is common
- Take personal responsibility
- Process any weakness
- Let go of things out of your control
- Grow through the pain
- Forgive
- Turn to others for help
- Share your story

Failure is never the end! It is, instead, a necessary part of the journey of life. This life can drain happiness right out of you if you let it. Your fear is what stops you from taking advantage of opportunities.

"Nothing in life is to be feared. It is only to be understood."
~ Marie Curie

FEAR:

False
Evidence
Appearing
Real

There is not one person on the planet that can satisfy everyone. It is not possible. So, allowing others to make you feel badly is something you want to avoid. If you make mistakes, you make mistakes! This does not mean that you are anything less than wonderful. You are not a failure. No one in life is perfect and everyone has had to learn in order for them to get where they are. Life is a total learning experience at every age level and continues throughout life.

The unknown is what creates discomfort and resistance. You have probably what-iffed yourself into a corner. We make decisions every day and we can only make a decision by the information we have at the time we make the decision. As we gain more experience, knowledge, or understanding, we may change our minds about some of the decisions we have made previously. That is normal!

What specific situations or events trigger your fear?

How does this fear impact your daily life, relationships, and goals?

So do not fear, for I am with you; do not be dismayed, for I am your God. I will strengthen you and help you; I will uphold you with my righteous right hand. (Isaiah 41:10 NIV)

5

Emotional Rollercoaster

Rageaholic

"A moment of patience in a moment of anger prevents a thousand moments." ~ Author Unknown

A rageaholic is someone who has a tendency to act out their anger in an extreme or inappropriate way. Some of the characteristics are: difficulty controlling their emotions (especially in a stressful situation), prone to physical altercations, quick to shout out, make long angry speeches, and verbal aggression.

There are really only two types of anger: your anger and other people's anger. Major research on anger has shown that people who are most prone to vent their rage get more angry, not less angry.

Anger is a tool you can use for good. It's not something to repress, deny, or fear. Anger is an alarm that tells you when a personal boundary is being violated or threatened. There are three major situations in which anger plays a good role:

1. As the protector of your self-worth
2. As the guardian of your convictions
3. As the announcer of your unmet needs

When you are deprived, exploited, manipulated, frustrated, betrayed, or humiliated, your self-worth is threatened. You get angry. Anger alerts you that you are being violated. Anger provides you with energy to act. But you must learn to control your anger and act in a positive and reasonable way.

You may tell yourself, "I am too sensitive...too childish." But in fact, you are under the attack of verbal abuse. Anger is the watchdog of your convictions; you need to take responsibility as to how you're going to react.

In all of these situations, anger can be a friend. But you must recognize your anger and use it to motivate you to take constructive steps to change the situation. If you don't, your anger will fester and you will only experience more anger.

Chronic anger can kill. When you allow anger to become the dominant emotion in your life, you slowly destroy yourself and often those around you. In addition, anger can interfere with your ability to concentrate and to solve problems.

Anger tends to feed on itself! When you act aggressively toward others, they may react aggressively towards you. Left unchecked, these responses can become a vicious cycle with a bad ending!

Many people relate anger to aggression and/or hostility. But anger is not aggression, anger is an emotion. Aggression is a course of action that a person chooses after experiencing anger. Somewhere between the motivation of your anger and your response, there is a choice. You can choose to use your anger constructively, or you can choose to abuse it. When you act aggressively towards others, you make yourself at once more isolated and more exposed. Expressing anger aggressively reveals your vulnerable points to others in ways that lead to more hurt rather than more understanding.

People who attempt to bury their anger go about their business unaware that their anger is operating at a subconscious level. They don't see their anger as the real cause of their "behavior" and neither do others.

You could say that being assertive is being proactive rather than reactive. When you react to events, you allow outside situations to control you. When you are proactive, you take responsibility for yourself.

You often hear the word "explode" used when someone is talking about someone getting very angry. Another term we should talk about is "implosion." This term is heard far less often, but when you repress or deny anger, you damage yourself on the inside. You take the anger out on yourself. Neither way of dealing with anger is a good option.

Unless you change something, the anger will always be there. In this case, being proactive might involve a long-term solution. Being proactive means looking at various options to correct whatever makes you feel so trapped. Anger doesn't go away until you change your situation. It's possible you are angry because that's what you learned to do. Ask yourself, are you dealing with old anger?

It takes courage, strength, and commitment to search out the unresolved events in your life and deal with them one by one. As long as those events remain unresolved, even if you don't "think" about them, they are an underground stream of anger that never dries up, keeping alive thorny vines that strangle your relationships and only does harm.

For some people, poor parental modeling, unresolved events, and irrational beliefs become twisted, making it even more difficult to sort out how much the past is interfering with their present functioning.

The key to getting over old anger is to realize that it's old. You can't go back and change your childhood so you need to use the anger for change. The second important consideration is to be safe; you don't want to hurt others or continue hurting yourself. You will not be able to resolve a childhood or a past relationship full of anger in a short time, but you can resolve it if you work at it. At some point and time of your life you can't blame everything on your childhood. Often childhood is an excuse that becomes overworked. Take responsibility for your here and now, and move forward.

How to recognize a Rageaholic:

1. They tend to take things personally and get offended easily
2. They're not afraid of conflict or confrontation
3. They always need an audience for their grievances
4. They blame others for their problems and never take responsibility for their actions
5. They're overly competitive and don't like to lose
6. They act in a way that's out of character for them when they're angry
7. They have a history of violence or abuse
8. They're prone to addictive behavior and anger is their drug of choice

How do you deal with a Rageaholic?

1. Don't ignore the problem
2. Don't let it get out of hand
3. Don't let it ruin your relationship with the rageaholic or anyone else you care about
4. Don't let it ruin your life, or the lives of those around you, who are also likely struggling with their own issues and trying to live as happy a life as best they can
5. Don't let this situation turn into an all-consuming whirlwind that sucks up every last drop of energy from both parties until there is nothing left but bitterness and regret
6. Seek professional help for all parties concerned

What causes one to become a Rageholic?

1. Growing up in a verbally or physically abusive environment
2. Growing up in an anger-filled environment
3. Having a family member with a history of rage
4. Differences in brain structure
5. Having a history of mental health disorders

How to manage your anger:

1. Acknowledge you're angry. Many people don't know they are angry until they blow up. To manage anger better, you must recognize that you have an anger issue.
2. Try to identify the specific event you are angry about. The more closely you can pinpoint the problem, the more likely you can resolve it.

3. At this point you make a conscious decision to use your anger as a tool rather than a weapon. When you use anger as a tool, you focus on it. When you use it as a weapon, you focus on the other person. You can always change yourself, but you cannot change others. Work on yourself and quit wasting time on others that you cannot change.

4. You need to carefully plan your reaction, not an off-the-cuff reaction at the moment you become angry.

5. A wise man once said, "No one begins a building or goes to war without finding out how much it is going to cost." Once you identify the problem and begin looking at solutions, count the cost. If you count the cost and decide it's still worth trying, you need to have some idea of how to proceed.

Often, your anger escalates because you think there is a motive to the other person's action. The problem is, it may or may not be the real motive. The mind is so powerful that it actually defines reality. It comes down to simply seeing the situation from another viewpoint.

When it is truly impossible or impractical for you to change a situation, you can change the way you perceive the situation. That is, you can change the way you think about it.

Once you acknowledge your anger and analyze why you are angry, you must deal with the situation as soon as possible. Resolve the situation and be done with it! But this isn't always that simple.

Humans detest change. The only one who likes change is a baby with a wet diaper. Whenever possible, we hold onto the old ways, no matter how painful they may be. But when change is needed, anger is truly your best friend. You CAN do "impossible" things if you put your anger to work.

When someone else is angry, it's easy to do one of two things: take flight, that is run away from the problem, or fight. These are the two natural reactions. If you let the other person's anger become your anger, chances are good that the situation won't be resolved. Try to de-escalate the anger.

Look objectively at the situation. Who is angry, and what about? By asking these questions, you can immediately put yourself outside of the storm. You are setting boundaries between you and the angry person.

A study shows that in a face-to-face encounter, 55 percent of what you communicate comes through body language. Your tone of voice communicates another 38 percent. Only 7 percent actually comes from the words you speak. The key is to have peace of mind. When your mind is at peace, your body language will reflect that.

Don't over apologize, but don't minimize the mistake or suggest that the other person "shouldn't feel that way." Saying "I'd feel the same way if I were in your position" is a lot better than "I know exactly how you feel." Even if you really do, most people believe their hurt or anger is unique.

Venting can be tough to listen to. But rarely does it take very long. Venting is a Latin word meaning "wind," and is usually over in a few minutes. You'll notice that the anger will lessen. Sanity will return in most cases. After the person has vented, focus on clarifying the cause of their anger. Tell them, "Let me see if I understand." Sometimes when they hear it being said back to them, they can recognize a solution on their own.

Silence can be a very powerful tool when you are dealing with angry people. Don't think you have to respond immediately to everything an angry person says. You may want to ask, "What is the solution you've thought of?"

You may be thinking, "So, I'm not allowed to get angry, but everyone else is allowed to do things they know will make me angry and then make excuses for it?" It doesn't matter how dirty others play; karma has a big bite. Always move with a genuine heart and pure intentions. There is no need for revenge because the person they are is already enough punishment.

"Before you argue with someone, ask yourself, is that person even mentally mature enough to grasp the concept of different perspectives? Because if not, there's absolutely no point."
~ Amber Veal

Every time you get upset about something ask yourself, "If I were to die tomorrow, was it worth wasting my time being angry and upset about this?" My favorite saying is, "100 years from now, many things won't matter!"

What triggers your anger most frequently?

**What ways have you found anger to be used
in a positive way?**

*"A gentle answer turns away wrath, but a harsh word
stirs up anger."* (Proverbs 15:1 NIV)

"Know this, my beloved brothers: let every person be quick to hear, slow to speak, slow to anger; for the anger of man does not produce the righteousness of God." (James 1: 19-20 ESV)

Stress and Anxiety

"There's a lot to think about, but nothing to worry about!"
~ Miracle Status

90% of what you worry about never happens!

"Worrying is like sitting in a rocking chair. It gives you something to do but it doesn't get you anywhere." ~ Corrie ten Boom

Butterflies rest when it rains because the water damages their wings. It's okay to rest during the storms of life. You'll fly again when they're over. Not everything happens in our timing, so be patient! Give yourself time to heal, don't push yourself.

What is stress? Stress is:

- External pressure that causes physical, mental or emotional strain.
- Self-induced internal stress that causes physical, emotional or spiritual strain.
- Internal resistance responding to outside pressure.
- Negative pressure that results in distress, danger, or destruction.
- Positive pressure producing motivation and movement.
- Our biological response to the pressure of life.

Most of your stress comes from the way you respond to life and not the way life really is. Adjust your attitude and leave that stress behind. Seventy percent of Americans admit to stress in their lives; 30 percent are actively trying to cut stress. Seventy-five percent of all doctors' visits are stress related. Here are a few of the most common stress-related disorders:

- Mental disorders
- Headaches
- TMJ
- Fibromyalgia
- Irritable bowel syndrome
- Neurodermatitis
- Eating disorder
- Substance abuse
- Immune system disorders

The seven classic causes and remedies of stress:

1. **Conflict** – accept one another's differences and focus on common goals. Speak openly and honestly in relationships.
2. **Crisis** – rely on God's comfort and peace when blindsided by trauma.
3. **Change** – welcome change as an opportunity to learn and grow.
4. **Condemnation** – expect to be rejected just as Jesus was rejected. Extend forgiveness and speak the truth in love.
5. **Concerns** – trust God with tomorrow and enjoy life today. Put away perfectionism and focus on improvement while aiming for excellence.

6. **Competition** – base your personal acceptance on being accepted by Christ.
7. **Conscience** – turn to God as the resource for meeting every need.

Nothing drains your energy faster than your own thoughts. Stop stressing over what's beyond your control. Protect your peace. Nothing is permanent. Don't stress too much because no matter how bad the situation is, it will change. Tell yourself, "Today I will not stress over things I can't control." A secret to happiness is letting every situation be what it is instead of what you think it should be and then making the best of it.

Don't try to build a life with no problems or stress. Build yourself into a person who can handle stress and solve problems. There is big difference. Anxiety comes from trying to do it all on your own. Peace comes from putting it all in God's hands. Anxiety is often a reaction to living too far in the future. Come back to the now, where your feet are, where your breath is, where your power lives.

Mental stress is caused by the way we think about or interpret events. Emotional stress is caused by the way we process our thoughts. Physical stress is caused by the way our bodies automatically respond to external pressure. Spiritual stress is caused by the way we view God, His involvement in our lives, and His sovereignty over our lives.

Flexible people are happy people. They experience a lot less stress than those who are rigid, those who insist on things always being done according to policy and exactly the way they have decided things should be done. One of the reasons that inflexibility is so stressful is that we have to achieve our goals and purposes through thinking humans who often have their own bright ideas. However, there are times you must follow protocol!

Life gets easier when you stop fighting it. The rain will fall whether you complain or not. Traffic will exist whether you stress or not. People will act how they want whether you worry or not. Focus on what you can change. Don't worry about the things you can't control. Let go of what you can't change. Sometimes you just have to pray, put it in God's hands, and leave it alone. Pray about it tonight then leave it alone.

Stress is a big emotional hurdle many of us face daily. RELAX. Ninety percent of what you worry about never happens! Seventy five to ninety percent of all doctor visits are stress related and stress is responsible for seventy to eighty percent of the disease in America. Stress is the most researched topic that battles against wellness. Six out of ten Americans feel overstressed, so you're not alone. Surround yourself with people of great wisdom and roll with it.

Distance yourself from the people who bring out the stress in you and move closer to those who bring out the best in you. Conflict is stressful, and it is to our advantage to keep it at bay. But we cannot eliminate all conflicts from our lives because we are all unique individuals with different backgrounds, communication styles, and preferences.

The positive influence of laughter on stress is well documented. Studies show that laughter lowers blood pressure and reduces hypertension. It reduces stress hormones and cleanses the lungs and body tissues of accumulated stale air because laughter empties more air out than it takes in. It boosts immune functions in the body.

Don't allow life's pressures and negative circumstances to snuff out your sense of humor. Laughter reflects positive emotions and makes you a lot more fun to be around. We have to learn how to roll with the punches. That's easier said than done!

Did you know you can remove a significant amount of stress from your life simply by reducing the number of items in your closet? Do you find yourself standing in front of your closet in the early morning, trying to make a decision on what to wear? The longer you stand there, sometimes the harder the decision is to make.

Stress, anxiety, and depression are caused when we live to please others. Stress makes you think that everything has to be fixed now. Stress and anxiety cause heart palpitations, headaches, acid reflux, insomnia, and more. Just breathe. Things have a way of working themselves out.

"Be kind to yourself. It's okay to rest." ~ Mother Teresa

Damages of stress:

- Stress is highly correlated with many physical problems such as heart disease, high blood pressure, and diabetes
- Treatments of these diseases now include stress management strategies/plans
- Stress impacts relationships with others
- Stress is responsible for seventy to eighty percent of the disease in America
- Seventy-five to ninety percent of all doctor's visits are stress related

Good Stress Prevention:

a. Learn how to recognize the stress-producing areas in your life
b. Learn how to rest
c. Learn how to renew your mind
d. Learn to be silent and learn to be still
e. Learn to give your burdens to God every day.
f. Learn to manage your time by saying "NO!"
g. Learn to resolve the things that you can attend to easily and quickly
h. Learn to delegate whenever appropriate
i. Exercise burns off adrenaline hormones
j. Proper nutrition
k. Proper sleep
l. Live in the moment

Stress is what you feel when you have to handle more than you are used to. It speeds up your heart, makes you breathe faster, and gives you short-term bursts of energy. There are many ways to manage stress and improve your overall health at the same time, such as:

- Determine what is causing the stress in your life and face it
- Be honest about what helps reduce stress and what doesn't
- Find better ways to cope with your stress, like exercise
- Try out new ways to relieve the harmful effects of stress
- Prioritize tasks and use a schedule to better manage your time
- Eliminate or delegate trivial tasks that increase your stress
- Take care of yourself and ask for help when you need it
- Rest, eat healthy foods, don't smoke, and limit your alcohol consumption

- Work on letting go of the things you can't change
- Learn to say "no" to things you can't or don't want to do
- Explain your needs and concerns to others to help relieve stress
- Communicate your feelings to others thoughtfully and tactfully

Steps to help reduce stress:

- **Recognize your worry** – write it down as it helps to see it on paper
- **Do a reality check** – what are the chances that this worry will actually happen
- **Physical activity** – an excellent stress buster and critical to normalizing your body after a stressful event
- **Make a plan** – putting action steps in place will help you handle the situation
- **Relax your body and mind** – turn it over to God. Scripture says be anxious of nothing (Philippians 4:6) and to cast our cares upon him. (1 Peter 5:7)

God's warning signs are much like road signs. They give you notice of change or danger.

- **STOP** – stop and look at the real reason you are experiencing stress
- **YIELD** – yield to God's sovereign control over your circumstances
- **RESUME SPEED** – living in the presence of God

When things feel overwhelming, remember:

One **THOUGHT** at a time
One **TASK** at a time
One **DAY** at a time

Have you caught yourself saying, "I just can't deal with this right now?" Life seems to be a steady juggling act. There are so many things we face daily that truly will not matter at the end of our life's journey. Don't waste your time or energy on everything that is thrown your way; concentrate on the things that really matter in life. If you can't do anything about it, then let it go. Don't be a prisoner to things you can't change.

Anxiety happens when you think you have to figure out everything all at once. Breathe. You're strong. You've got this. Take it one day at a time.

Keep the Power Ps as your guide:

Praise – things accomplished
Pressure – problems facing
Plan – what are you going to do

Here are just some of the symptoms that stress can trigger:

1. Tense muscles
2. Headaches
3. Gastrointestinal problems
4. Heart palpitations
5. Sleep problems
6. Weight gain

When we're stressed, we often look to food for comfort. In addition, the stress hormone cortisol, which increases when we are stressed, can lead to overeating and cause the body to store more fat.

Life is too short to stress yourself with people who don't even deserve to be an issue in your life.

The Serenity Prayer

**God, grant me the serenity
to accept the things I cannot change,
the courage to change the things I can,
and the wisdom to know the difference.**

How does stress and anxiety impact your daily life?

**What are your current coping mechanisms
for managing stress and anxiety?**

"Do not be anxious about anything, but in every situation, by prayer and petition, with thanksgiving, present your requests to God. And the peace of God, which transcends all understanding, will guard your hearts and your minds in Christ Jesus." (Philippians 4:6 NIV)

"Cast all your anxiety on him because he cares for you."
(1 Peter 5:7 NIV)

Setting Boundaries

"Daring to set boundaries is about having the courage to love ourselves, even when we risk disappointing others." ~ Brene Brown

Never feel guilty for setting boundaries that protect your peace! We are living in a day where people are proud of what they should be ashamed of.

What are boundaries? Boundaries are a dividing line, a line not to be crossed. Personal boundaries are like a fence protecting you from people, places, and priorities that are wrong. They protect you from people who want to take more than they should. Boundaries help form a healthy give-and-take relationship.

Have you noticed that everyone loves you when you let everything slide, but the moment you start setting boundaries and holding people accountable, you become the one that's difficult? Don't try to build a life with no problems or stress. Build yourself into a person who can handle stress and solve problems. There's a big difference!

Seeing all the different boundaries affecting our daily lives makes us aware that keeping boundaries set is an everyday challenge. These boundaries include physical, mental, emotional and spiritual boundaries. These dividing lines for our lives help us distinguish what our responsibility is and what it isn't.

Many people live scattered and fairy tale lives trying to live outside of their own boundaries, not accepting and expressing the truth of who they really are. Honesty about who you are gives you the biblical value of integrity or oneness. Sometimes physically removing yourself from a situation will help maintain your boundaries. God limited his exposure to evil, unrepentant people, as should we.

Establishing boundaries in our thinking involves three things:

1. We must own our own thoughts
2. We must grow in knowledge and expand our minds
3. We must clarify distorted thinking

Boundaries define us. They define what is me and what is not me. What a simple yet powerful statement! Many times, we find ourselves out of our boundary zone due to keeping peace in a relationship and not engaging in a conflict even though the conflict results doesn't define who we really are or what we stand for. God has boundaries and lives within his boundaries. Boundaries are a good thing!

Remember that a boundary always deals with you, not the other person. You are setting boundaries to say what you will do or will not do or tolerate. You should not demand that others do something either. Respect others' boundaries as well.

Boundaries need to be communicated first verbally and then with actions. They need to be clear and unapologetic. If you are hurting, you need to own that hurt. You only have the power to change yourself. You can't change other people. Keep your boundaries.

We need to continually challenge ourselves to learn new things. The same process that we use to drive a car, swim, or learn a foreign language is the one we use for learning better self-boundaries. Change is frightening. It may comfort you to know that if you are afraid, you are possibly on the right road—the road to change and growth.

Running into resistance is a good sign even though it doesn't seem like it. It's a sign that you are doing what you need to do. It will be worth it. Remember the clear message of the scriptures: "For you are receiving the end result of your faith, the salvation of your souls." (1 Peter 1:9 NIV)

The journey of life is always riddled with trouble, but also with the promises of our Shepherd to carry us through if we do our part. Go for it!! One of the signs that you're beginning to develop boundaries is a sense of resentment, frustration, or anger at the subtle and not-so-subtle violations in your life.

You will begin to see that taking responsibility for yourself is healthy, and you will begin to understand that taking responsibility for other adults is destructive.

For years, Christians have been taught that protecting their spiritual and emotional property is selfish. Yes, God is interested in people loving others, but you can't love others unless you love yourself. Setting boundaries is mature, proactive, and initiative taking. It's taking control of our lives with God's guidance.

Boundaries are a defensive tool, but they are sometimes seen as offensive tools. If boundaries are used correctly, they don't control, attack, or hurt anyone. Boundaries are for yourself; you are not setting anyone else's boundaries but your own. What a great thought! Often setting boundaries seems like we are trying to impose our thoughts or ideas onto someone else but this simply is not true.

Keeping our boundaries in check is something we have to work at for life. We must continue to improve our skills and never let our guard down. We also know there are two types of battles: outside resistance and inside resistance we get from ourselves. As the old saying goes, sometimes we are our own worst enemy!

Empathy without boundaries is self-destruction. Unconditional love doesn't mean unconditional tolerance. You have to train your boundaries to be stronger than your soft heart and your mind to be stronger than your feelings. Otherwise, you'll be drained. So be kind, but don't become a doormat that people can walk all over!

Remember, anger tells you that your boundaries have been violated. Not setting boundaries is like going outside when it rains and expecting to stay dry.

"I think so often, what people misunderstand about boundaries is that the point of setting them is not to change other people's behavior or convince then to value different things – it's to advocate for yourself, regardless of how they respond." ~ Daniel Koepke

Your boundaries are not making you lose friends or family members—your boundaries are making you lose gas-lighters, emotional abusers, needy and greedy manipulators, self-centered narcissists, and energy-draining vampires. Keep standing up for yourself – you're doing great.

Setting boundaries is not about being selfish. It's about being self-aware, self-respectful, and self-protective. It's about recognizing your own needs, your own feelings, and your own limitations, and being brave enough to communicate them to others.

Boundaries are not barriers, they're bridges. They're connections to yourself, to your own inner wisdom, and to your own emotional and psychological well-being. They're what separate healthy relationships from toxic ones, and what distinguish self-love from self-sacrifice.

So, don't let anyone make you feel guilty for setting boundaries. Don't let anyone convince you that you're being selfish or unreasonable, and don't let anyone manipulate you into compromising your own needs and feelings.

Remember, your boundaries are a reflection of your self-worth, your self-respect, and your self-love. They're a declaration of your own self-sufficiency, your own action, and your own dignity, so keep standing up for yourself, keep setting those boundaries, and keep loving yourself. You're doing great! We often tolerate a lot because we don't want to lose people, but now we need to realize that those people are not our people. Set boundaries and keep them!

There are times we enforce our boundaries knowing it could cost us a relationship. God never gave us the power or the right to control how others respond to our "no." This is a tough concept to overcome, but we also know we must take a stand and simply say "no" at times. Keep in mind, it is typically self-centered people who get angry when someone tells them no! No one has the power to make you feel guilty. Do not let guilt be your master any longer.

Keep standing up for yourself; you're doing exactly what you need to do. Having clear boundaries is essential to a healthy, balanced lifestyle.

Dr. Cloud and Dr. Townsend state in their book, *Boundaries: When to say Yes, How to say No*, to take control of your life. "Boundaries define us. They define what is me and what is not." We are faced with boundary decisions in our daily lives and keeping our boundaries set is a lifelong challenge regardless of age.

Don't wait for things to get better. Life will always be complicated. Learn to be happy right now or you'll run out of time. Time passes quickly and not one of us knows how long we will live.

"Life is all about balance. You don't always need to be getting stuff done. Sometimes it's perfectly okay, and absolutely necessary, to shut down, kick back, and do nothing." ~ Lori Deschene

Stop giving people more chances to disappoint you. Move on! We don't distance ourselves from people to teach them a lesson; we distance ourselves because we finally learned ours. Be careful. When you do too much for people, they start loving your hand, not your heart.

Keeping our boundaries in check is something we have to work at for life. Surround yourself with loving and supportive people; we all need a strong support system. Often people who are successful and keep healthy boundaries are viewed as being selfish or self-centered. You should never feel guilty about maintaining healthy boundaries. Many times, the people who express boundaries as being selfish or self-centered are the people who can no longer successfully manipulate you.

"If you invite someone into your home and they start breaking things and insulting your décor, you don't have to hate them, but you wouldn't invite them into your home anymore. Boundaries are doing the same thing except your home is your mind. Your home is your heart. Your home is your time and your life. Uninvite the guests who don't know how to treat your home with respect." ~ Doe Zantamata

Unhealthy relationships generally reflect a failure to understand and work within appropriate boundaries. Since unhealthy boundaries are almost always the result of being raised in some variation of a dysfunctional family, the likelihood children raised in such families will develop healthy boundaries is limited.

How to build strong boundary limits:

1. **Place boundaries around your heart** – be careful where and on whom you spend your emotions.
2. **Learn that it's okay to say no** – do not listen to lies about being selfish or uncaring when you refuse to comply with someone's wishes.
3. **Start being assertive** – nonassertive behavior allows others to violate your personal rights; by your behavior you actually permit the violation.
4. **Draw the line** – to help identify your boundaries, pay attention when your emotions are intense, dark, shaming, or guilt-ridden in response to something someone has said or done to you. Is someone crossing your boundary line?
5. **Appropriate God's will for your life** – begin to redefine your own, separate identity by daily choosing to live according to God's will.

God's desire is for you to know where your injuries and shortfalls are, whether self-induced or induced by others. Boundary development is essential in the earlier years of life, but many of us don't know the importance of boundaries at that point in life. Boundaries are sometimes seen as an offensive weapon rather than a defensive tool.

Where in your life do you need to set boundaries?

"For each will have to bear his own load." (Galatians 6:5 ESV)

"Make no friendship with a man given to anger, nor go with a wrathful man, lest you learn his ways and entangle yourself in a snare." (Proverbs 22:24-25 ESV)

"Whoever walks with the wise becomes wise, but the companion of fools will suffer harm." (Proverbs 13:20 ESV)

6

Dealing With Rejection

"If rejection is the curse, confidence is the cure!" ~ Author Unknown

"Don't be upset when people reject you. Nice things are rejected all the time by people who can't afford them." ~ Author Unknown

Rejection is one of the strongest emotional challenges! Most people face some sort of rejection throughout their lifetime to some degree or another. Rejection sends us on a mission to seek and destroy our self-esteem. Blaming ourselves and attacking our self-worth only deepens the emotional pain we feel and makes it harder for us to recover emotionally. When you experience rejection, you feel unloved, unwanted, and unacceptable.

There are three levels of acceptance:

1. **Zero Acceptance** – No matter what I do, I'll never be accepted or good enough.
2. **Performance-based acceptance** – I feel accepted only when I perform perfectly.
3. **Unconditional acceptance** – No matter what I do, even when I fail, I always feel accepted.

Even if rejection is slight, it can be enough to cause you to question your self-worth. Don't accept self-criticism. Rebuild your self-worth by focusing on your strengths, finding other people to fill the void, and desensitizing yourself to the pain of future rejection through practice sessions in which you set yourself up for mild rejections that you can readily overcome.

I think back to when my family went on family vacations. Believe me, it didn't happen too often when there were six kids and two adults! All eight of us rode in a standard car, so it was a tight ride. Two different times I remember my next oldest sister and I were told we would not be going on vacation with the family, that we would need to find a place to stay. We both felt totally rejected. Everyone else got to go on vacation and we had to find a place to stay.

People who know their value do not compare themselves with others. There's a hidden beauty in being rejected, misunderstood, unseen, and unsupported by people. It teaches you to rely on God for everything.

The ABC's of Rejection:

> Accept the facts
> Believe the truth
> Change your behavior

Letting go of grudges and bitterness can make way for happiness, health, and peace. Cry until you laugh if you need to! Laughter is good for your soul and great medicine. Don't focus on the shortcomings or the limitations of your circumstances. Rather, look to God to make a way.

Suffering In Silence

Rejection and failure are very closely related. If you feel controlled by the fear of rejection, then your focus is on people pleasing. 1 Thessalonians 2:4 clearly tells us that we are not trying to please men but God.

The feeling of rejection can subtly creep into our lives and attack our minds and emotions. Rejection can alter our own self-perception and bring on the inevitable self-doubt that seems to take hold when someone painfully rejects you. Rejection can hit hard. It can not only attack your mind but taint your thoughts and even make you question your own abilities to the point of not being able to function normally.

The saddest part of rejection is it breeds rejection. No one can avoid being rejected or treated unfairly at times. That's when we must remember our identity is in the Lord. He created us in His image.

How we live our lives is based on what we believe. Therefore, if we believe we are rejected, we will live a life of rejection in our minds, our hearts, and our emotions, even when we are not outwardly rejected by others. Since people do fail people, it is essential not to let other people define who you are. Rejection can be a horrible mind game!

Accept rejection

Don't beg

Never chase

Know your worth

Choose yourself

We all can form a self-pity party pretty quickly when we experience rejection. It may go something like this:

- I should have never been born
- I was never wanted
- I will never amount to a thing

Many of us have heard or thought those phrases, but you can't dwell on them.

Rejection can come in many forms. It could be a huge blow, like a partner being unfaithful, to a loved one moving out and calling off a relationship for good. The way we handle rejection is important in helping us keep our self-esteem and dignity.

Being rejected hurts. The person you entrusted with your hopes, desires, and feelings has turned around and said that they don't want to be involved with you. Rejection and lack of honesty go hand in hand. Rejection can come from many sources: parents, siblings, a spouse, a boss or friends.

Rejection destabilizes our "need to belong." We feel alone and disconnected after a rejection. Rejection can create surges of anger and aggression. Research shows even mild rejections lead people to take out their aggression on innocent bystanders.

"Every time I thought I was being rejected from something good,
I was actually being re-directed to something better."
~ Dr. Steve Marabali

Painful Rejection

"The people who wound us get no say in how we clean up the blood."
~ Author Unknown

Rejection and physical pain connect pathways in the brain. The brain becomes activated when we experience rejection in the same manner as when we experience physical pain. This is called social pain. We can relive and re-experience social pain more vividly than we can physical pain. Social pain connects with our feelings, which makes it much easier for us to remember rejection.

Rejection temporarily lowers our IQ. When we are reeling from a painful rejection, thinking clearly is just not that easy. Rejection does not respond to reason. Removing your presence from places you don't feel loved, valued, or respected is top-tier self-care. Give yourself time to think the situation through before you blurt out or react with any type of response.

If you live in the past and allow past rejection to define who you are, then you will never grow. We tend to focus on our shortcomings or the limitations of our circumstances rather than looking to God to make a way.

"There are people who have to see you as the problem, because if you're the problem it means they're not; and if they're not the problem then that means they don't have to change anything."
~ Mark Smith

People these days don't apologize for doing wrong. Rather, they blame others for how they react.

I can do all things through Christ who strengthens me.
(Philippians 4:13 NKJV)

Root of Rejection

Rejection is an issue most people face to some degree or another. It is also the reason they reach out for counseling more today than ever before. Throughout our lifetime, we all will be faced with some sort of rejection. Rejection can be very painful if we allow it to be.

But first we must figure out what the cause of the rejection is. There can be many sources related to rejection: abuse, turmoil, home life, family dynamics, abandonment, adoption, unfaithful marriage, peers, co-workers, bosses, etc.

We are to uproot from the old ways and wrong things and be replanted in all the right things. Many times, we feel like we do the uprooting but forget to replant, thus allowing our old roots to take hold again and flourish. We cannot let other people determine our worth; we must take responsibility and take charge of our lives. There may be instances where people reject your ideas, but that doesn't mean they are rejecting you.

We are blood-brought through Christ Jesus and have the right to take full command of our lives and futures. However, we are human and when we come up against the feeling of rejection our first instinct is to get angry, defensive, and want to get even. Rejection is one of Satan's favorite tools to use; he knows it cuts deep and sharp. He also knows how to keep opening the old wounds.

God wants to build a wall of protection around us. We are his children. God does not want to see us hurt or get hurt. When we let God do his job in our lives, we then make progress. Our part is to believe; his part is to do.

We can't dwell or focus on the things we didn't do right. We need to keep on keeping on if we want to make progress. Our goal as a Christian is to become Christ-like; we can't get stuck on all our past mistakes. We need to seek forgiveness and move forward. God loves us unconditionally; we don't have to spend time getting God to like us!

We reject ourselves and others because of imperfections; others reject us due to imperfections. Joyce Meyer states, "God never rejects us because of our imperfections or weaknesses. DEPEND on GOD."

It is so easy for one to get caught up in the perfection mode of life. We wait until everything appears to be perfect and find ourselves continuing to still wait on perfection. God doesn't require us to have everything perfect in life. Some progress is better than no progress at all.

Often we find ourselves in a situation or a conversation giving a response to other people based on what we ourselves need. We try to give people the very same thing we need ourselves. If we are looking for people to always agree with us, that is not healthy communication but manipulation. We can learn so much from other people. We need to be open to hear what they have to say.

The central theme we all must hold onto when dealing with rejection is this: people may reject us but God will never reject us. Let's desire popularity with God above popularity with people.

What are the root causes of rejection?

- Past traumatic experiences
- Social comparison
- Low self-esteem
- Perfectionist mindset
- Societal influence
- Negative thought pattern

Nine tips on how to overcome the fear of rejection:

- Accept that rejection is a normal part of life
- Challenge your negative thoughts about rejection
- Write down the worst outcome of any negative thoughts and accept it
- Face your fear
- Develop a growth mindset
- Cultivate resilience
- Practice positive affirmations
- Practice visualization every day
- Go for professional help

How do you handle rejection?

What are some of your struggles with rejection?

"If the world hates you, keep in mind that it hated me first."
(John 15:18 NIV)

For the Lord will not reject his people; he will never forsake his inheritance. (Psalms 94:14 NIV)

7

Money Does Matter

"Too many people spend money they earned...to buy things they don't want...to impress people that they don't like." ~ Will Rogers

"A wise person should have money in their head, but not in their heart." ~ Jonathan Swift

Money is a key factor in many aspects of life and existence. However, some use money for power. Money isn't the most important thing, but it is important. We all need a certain amount of money to survive but money is just a tool to achieve what you need. Money does not buy happiness, good health, or importance in society.

No matter how it is used, money itself does not make decisions. People make decisions as to how they use their money. Some decisions are wise and others we find to not be so wise.

Financial boundaries help you:

- Responsibly manage your budget and accounting procedures
- Responsibly manage your spending and savings
- Responsibly pay bills and meet other financial obligations on time
- Responsibly make investments for the future

- Responsibly make wills or trusts that place restrictions on how others use your resources

Some people have in their minds that spoiling a woman is about money, but that is not true. It includes time, attention, and being there emotionally, physically, and mentally. The money comes and goes but how she is made to feel is forever.

What are your financial habits?

- Do you get cash advances from credit cards to pay other expenses?
- Do you pay only the minimum on credit card balances?
- Do you bounce checks or overdraw your bank account?
- Do you ignore the importance of having a savings account steadily accruing money?
- Do you use savings to pay credit card bills?
- Do you send in payments past the due date?
- Do you avoid opening mail?
- Do you wait until the last minute to pay taxes?
- Do you have family conflicts over money?

If you answer yes to any of the questions above, you will need to make some adjustments to increase your financial freedom. Financial freedom means enough income, savings, and investments to afford the lifestyle you desire without relying solely on a job for income. Financial freedom is where you have control over your finances in order to make good choices to reach your goals.

Spend/Save

Any money you spend eating well, dressing well, and exploring
the world is never a waste, providing you have the funds available.
Don't spend more than you can make—we are to be good stewards
of our money!

**There are a number of contributing factors and lifestyles
that can lead you to debt:**

- Using money to keep up your social status
- Using money to make you feel important
- Using money to manipulate others
- Spending money to lift your spirits (retail therapy)
- Spending money to buy love or affection
- Spending money due to obsession with possessions
- Seeking gain without working for it
- Borrowing through means of credit cards
- Failing to take financial responsibility
- Failing to establish a budget and follow it
- Neglecting to pay off debts
- Neglecting to save for the future

There are basically two types of debt: intelligent borrowing such as a
home mortgage and stupid debt, such as credit cards and installment
loans. People need to debt-proof their lives to survive lean times
and help reduce stress. People need to learn the difference between
needs and wants. Many people use the phrase, "I deserve this or that."
Frankly, that is an emotional factor to decision making which is not a
wise position to put yourself in.

Six signs that someone is headed for the debt-trap:

- Living on credit cards instead of cash
- Delaying payment or paying late
- Unwilling or unable to save or give
- Unable to pay taxes
- Living an extravagant lifestyle
- Looking for get-rich-quick ideas

Before you make any purchase, you should ask yourself:

- Is this purchase a need or a want?
- Do I have adequate funds to purchase this without using credit?
- Have I comparison shopped?
- Does my spouse agree with me (if you are married) about making this purchase?
- Do I have God's peace regarding this purchase? Are my tithes current?

Take a minute to identify your debt inventory!

- What do you own?
- What do you owe?
- How much money do you make?
- What are your fixed expenses?
- What are your variable expenses?
- How does your monthly budget look and what spending does it allow?
- What are my financial goals now and for the future?

Here are some simple common sense money rules:

- If you don't need it, do not buy it.
- If you can cook it, don't order it.
- If your public library has it, don't purchase it.
- If you can use an older one, don't buy a newer one.
- If you can use a cheaper one, don't buy a costly one.
- If you can't pay cash for it, don't buy it.
- If you can repair it, don't replace it.
- If you can still use it, don't get rid of it.

Dave Ramsey developed what he calls **"The Seven Baby Steps"** to becoming debt-free:

Step One – Deposit $1,000 to start an emergency fund

Step Two – Pay off all debts using the Debt Snowball, eliminating the smallest debt first then applying that payment toward the next smallest

Step Three – Place three to six months of expenses in savings

Step Four – Invest 15 percent of household income into Roth IRAs and pre-tax retirement accounts

Step Five – Begin a college fund for children

Step Six – Pay off your home early

Step Seven – Build wealth and give accordingly

10 Strategies to Master Your Money
by Valorie Burton

1. Identify past choices that have led to financial frustration or stress – and stop making those choices, starting today.
2. Pay off credit cards before other debt.
3. Stop using your credit cards unless you can trust yourself to pay them in full each month.
4. Change your lifestyle if necessary.
5. Get insurance (health, life, home or renters, auto, and disability) that you feel confident will meet your needs in the event you need to use it.
6. Establish a financial cushion of six to 12 months of expenses.
7. Invest time in your own financial education.
8. Refuse to be an emotional spender.
9. Have a vision. Set goals!
10. Put money into proper perspective.

Financial Abuse

Financial friction and uncertainties are among the most frequent stressors and causes of breakdowns in relationships. Whether subtle or obvious, there are common methods that abusers use to gain financial control over their partner. These include:

- Forbidding the victim from attending job training or advancement opportunities
- Controlling how all of the money is spent
- Not including the victim in investment or banking decisions

- Not allowing the victim access to bank accounts
- Withholding money or giving "an allowance"
- Forcing the victim to write bad checks or file fraudulent tax returns
- Running up substantial amounts of debt on joint accounts
- Refusing to work or contribute to the family income
- Withholding funds for the victim or children to obtain basic needs such as food and medicine
- Hiding assets
- Stealing the victim's identity, property, or inheritance
- Forcing the victim to work in a family business without pay
- Refusing to pay bills and ruining the victim's credit score
- Forcing the victim to turn over public benefits or threatening to turn the victim in for "cheating or misusing benefits"
- Filing false insurance claims
- Refusing to pay or evading child support, or manipulating the divorce process by drawing it out by hiding or not disclosing assets
- Forbidding the victim to work. Sabotaging work or employment opportunities by stalking or harassing the victim at the workplace

Financial abuse is often the first sign of dating violence and/or domestic abuse. Financial abuse occurs in 99 percent of domestic violence cases in America, with 85 percent of them being women! That's why identifying financial abuse is critical to your safety and security. It is characterized by attempts to control, use, or manage your financial resources. The abuser may take your money, control your ability to earn money, or create debt in your name, among other things.

Financial abuse involves controlling a victim's ability to acquire, use, and maintain financial resources. Those who are victimized financially may be prevented from working, or the abuser may attempt to control how they use the money they earn. Some abusers want you to manage all of the household funds so they can put blame on you when things become tight!

While less commonly understood than other forms of abuse, financial abuse is one of the most powerful methods of keeping a victim trapped in an abusive relationship. Research shows that victims often are too concerned about their ability to provide financially for themselves and their children to end the relationship. Financial insecurity is also one of the top reasons women return to an abusive partner.

Men can be victims of abuse as well. Because financial abuse is recognized as a form of domestic violence, approximately 1 in 7 men (18 years and older) will experience a form of domestic violence.

Like other forms of intimate partner violence, the goal of financial abuse is to gain power and control in a relationship. When a dating partner or spouse uses or controls the money you have earned or saved, they are abusing your resources.

Here are some examples of this exploitation:

- Controlling or spending your money
- Ruining your credit history
- Feeling entitled to your money or assets
- Interfering with your finances

When a spouse has complete control over the money in the relationship and you have little or no access to what you need, this is controlling the family resources. Here are some examples of controlling shared resources and assets:

- **Criticizing every financial decision you make** and requiring you to account for every penny you spend (may even ask for receipts and change)
- **Having a double standard when it comes to their spending** (they may spend money on entertainment, dining out, and clothing but criticize you when you make similar purchases)
- **Making significant financial decisions without your input**, refusing to collaborate on finances, and limiting your access to the overall financial picture as a couple
- **Limiting your access to money** by not allowing you to have bank accounts or credit cards, or by withholding financial information such as account passwords, account numbers, and investment information
- **Hiding or taking funds** and putting them in a private account, insisting you share your income but refusing to share theirs, or refusing to work or contribute to the family income
- **Controlling the "purse strings,"** forcing you to ask for money, or establishing unrealistic limits or allowances
- **Demanding that you ask permission before spending money** but not consulting you when they make purchases, and requiring that large, joint purchases be in their name only (such as car loans, mortgages, cell phones, or apartment leases)

- **Becoming enraged over money** and then engaging in other forms of abuse like name-calling or physical violence
- **Evading or refusing to pay child support** and dragging out divorce proceedings to cripple you financially

When a spouse attempts to control your ability to earn money or gain assets, they are interfering with your income potential. Here are some examples of job interference:

- Criticizing and minimizing your job or choice of career
- Pressuring you to quit your job—sometimes even using children as an excuse
- Telling you where you can and cannot work
- Sabotaging your work responsibilities
- Harassing you at work by calling, texting, or stopping by
- Preventing you from working by hiding your keys, unhooking your car battery, taking your car without permission, or offering to babysit and then not showing up
- Forcing you to work for a family business without compensation or benefits

Financial abuse doesn't always look the same. Sometimes an abuser may use subtle tactics like manipulation, while other abusers may be more obvious, demanding, and intimidating. There is also the case where one of the partners doesn't want anything to do with the household finances. Their check is in the bank and you take care of everything from there. But some people use this as a way to pass the blame should things not go well with their finances.

De-cluttering Your Finances

1. **Create a Simple Budget** – get a better handle on your cash flow
2. **Establish a Bill-paying Plan** – financial pros say it's better to schedule a monthly, or even biweekly, block of time to review and pay bills.
3. **Keep Bill Storage Simple** – get an accordion file folder with 13 pockets, label each divider with the months leaving one for taxes.
4. **What to keep:**
   - **One Year:** Paycheck stubs, utility bills, canceled checks, credit cards receipts, bank statements
   - **Seven Years:** Brokerage statements; receipts, cancelled checks, and other documents that support income or deductions on your tax returns; purchase confirmations and 1099s
   - **Hold while active:** contracts, insurance documents, stock certificates, property records, warranties, stock records, records of pensions and retirement plans, property tax records, disputed bills, home improvement records
   - **Keep Forever:** life insurance policies, wills, mortgage records, income tax returns (you may need them when it comes time to draw Social Security as their records are not always accurate)

Future/Retirement

The aging process is inevitable but how we choose to handle the changes through the process is up to us. By 2030 there will be 71 million Americans older than 65 years of age. In the next 25 years, the US population over the age of 65 will have doubled. Financial security in retirement doesn't just happen. It takes a lot of thought and planning.

Top 10 Ways to Prepare for Retirement:

1) **Start saving, keep saving, and stick to your goals.** If you are already saving, whether for retirement or another goal, keep going!

2) **Know your retirement needs because retirement is expensive.** Experts estimate that you will need 70 to 90 percent of your preretirement income to maintain your standard of living when you stop working.

3) **Contribute to your employer's retirement savings plan.** If your employer offers a retirement savings plan, such as a 401(k) plan, sign up and contribute all you can.

4) **Learn about your employer's pension plan.** If your employer has a traditional pension plan, check to see if you are covered by the plan and understand how it works.

5) **Consider basic investment principles.** How you save can be as important as how much you save. Know how your savings or pension plan is invested. Inflation and the type of investments you make play important roles in how much you'll have saved at retirement.

6) **Don't touch your retirement savings.** If you withdraw your retirement savings now, you'll lose principal and interest, and you may lose tax benefits or have to pay withdrawal penalties.

7) **Ask your employer to start a plan.** If your employer doesn't offer a retirement plan, suggest that it start one.

8) **Put money into an Individual Retirement Account.** You can put up to $6,500 a year into an Individual Retirement Account (IRA); you can contribute even more if you are 50 or older.

9) **Find out about your Social Security benefits.** On average, Social Security retirement benefits replace 40 percent of pre-retirement income for retirement beneficiaries.

10) **Ask questions and make sure you understand the answers to those questions.** Get practical advice and act now.

20 common questions most people will face in retirement by Peter Kinzler

1. What triggers recognition that your life has an expiration date?
2. When should you retire?
3. Do you have enough money to retire?
4. What can you do if you haven't saved enough money?
5. How will you make your money last? Devise a sound investment strategy.
6. How will you make your money stretch? Know and manage your expenses.

7. How do you and your spouse share physical space in the house?
8. What will you do with your new-found time?
9. If work has been very important, how do you handle not being part of that world?
10. How do you make sense of your life?
11. How will you handle the physical limitations that come with aging?
12. How will you handle any regrets?
13. How will you deal with being treated as an older person?
14. How will your relationship with your children change, now that they are grown up and you are beyond grown up?
15. What kind of relationship do you want to have with your grandchildren?
16. What special things will you leave to your children?
17. What do you want to leave your children in terms of knowledge of yourself and their ancestors?
18. What do you need to do to put your financial affairs in order?
19. How will you decide when, if ever, it is time to leave your home?
20. How can you retain your sense of humor?

Pre-Retirement Checklist:

Do not wait until the last minute to start planning for your retirement. What follows is a list of nine things you can do prior to retirement that will make your golden years shine:

1. Pay off your mortgage and any other debt
2. Coordinate with your spouse

3. Determine what your vision is for your retirement
4. Create a realistic retirement budget
5. Assess the resources available to fund your retirement
6. Test drive your retirement
7. Assess your asset allocation
8. Determine how you will cover health care costs
9. Protect yourself and your assets with long-term care insurance

Do you have a budget?

How well does it align with your income and expenses?

"Keep your lives free from the love of money and be content with what you have..." (Hebrews 13:5 NIV)

Whoever loves money never has enough; whoever loves wealth is never satisfied with their income. This too is meaningless. (Ecclesiastes 5:10 NIV)

Dishonest money dwindles away, but whoever gathers money little by little makes it grow. (Proverbs 13:11 NIV)

8
Moving Forward

"Do not wish to be anything but what you are and try to be that perfectly." ~ St Francis De Sales

Don't look back when you are moving forward! Your rearview mirror is smaller than your windshield so you can keep moving forward with a clear view!

Believe in Yourself

"When a train goes through a tunnel and it gets dark, you don't throw away the ticket and jump off. You sit still and trust the engineer." ~ Corrie Ten Boom

Take total responsibility for everything that has happened to you so far, because if you don't, you will never be able to make real changes. Unless you want to live the rest of your days conforming to societal norms (whatever that might be), you will need to learn to get into the driver seat and take charge of your life. Any lesson you refuse to learn will repeat itself until you do. It may take a lot of courage, but you have to take full responsibility and tell yourself that...

"I am where I am because I let myself get here."

Don't change so people will like you. Be yourself and the right people will love the real you. The strongest people aren't always the people who win, but the people who don't give up when they lose.

We have to keep going. Even when it's scary, even when all of our strength seems gone, we have to keep picking ourselves back up and move forward, because whatever we're battling in the moment, it will pass and we will make it through. We've made it this far. We can make it through whatever comes next.

Don't let your outer circumstances determine your reality...

Stop being a slave to your mind and start deciding how you want to live.

Some people don't like you because you're exactly who you say you are. Meanwhile, they have to pick and choose which mask they're going to wear each day. Walk away from people who put you down and wear a mask! Walk away from fights that will never be solved. Walk away from trying to please people who will never see your worth. The more you walk away from things that poison your soul, the healthier you will be.

People who take charge of their lives and mold them into the type of lifestyle they want aren't affected by what other people tell them. Instead, they listen to their inner gut and go by what feels right for them.

"Failure doesn't mean the game is over... it means you get to try again with experience." ~ Dani Johnson

Successful people choose to do what they want to do, rather than what they think they have to do. If you want to begin to really take charge of your life and direct it in the right way so you can build a lifestyle many would die for, you must learn to take responsibility for everything—the good, the bad, and the ugly! Your life is yours to live and no one else's, so choose what you want to go for and put everything else secondary. Remember, there is a difference between being self-centered and being successful.

"Success is the sum of small efforts, repeated day in and day out."
~ Robert Collier

"Society has gotten to the point where everybody has a right but nobody has a responsibility." ~ Unknown

No one is responsible for your happiness but yourself. No one else can make you happy but you. You will never make any changes to your life or make progress in life if you don't take full responsibility for your life. It is too easy to conform to what society calls "the norm," although I'm not sure there is such a thing in the world today!

Someone once said, "most of the world is asleep, and only a few are awake." Are you asleep or awake? Are you in the driver's seat or are you a passenger just passing through life, sightseeing and following the herd?

We make many decisions every day of our lives and with every decision, we must be willing to be responsible for the consequences of our decisions. Decisions should be made with research—don't just follow the herd! Do your homework and research the situations you are facing. Don't rely on other people's opinions.

"You are responsible for your own happiness. If you expect others to make you happy, you will always be disappointed."
~ Author Unknown

Granted that some decisions bring greater consequences than others, yet great or small, we must claim responsibility for those decisions.

"Freedom is the will to be responsible to ourselves."
~ Friedrich Nietzsche

With most decisions ACTION needs to take place. Again, we must take responsibility for our actions. Do you find yourself setting goals and then forgetting about them or getting sidetracked? Don't give up—sit down, refocus, and get yourself back on track to moving forward. There will always be many circumstances we encounter in life that try to throw us off course, even to the point of sometimes knocking us down. Get up, brush yourself off, and get moving!

"The willingness to accept responsibility for one's own life is the source from which self-respect springs." ~ Joan Didion

Self-Respect

Self-respect is pride and confidence in one self, a feeling that one is behaving with honor and dignity. To have self-respect is to take care of yourself for who you are, to wake up and forgive yourself for mistakes you have made. View yourself in a positive way.

Some ways to help build a stronger self-respect:

1. Don't let people's thoughts about you shape who you are.
2. Don't let anybody force you to be or do anything you don't want to do simply for their approval or friendship.
3. Don't speak badly about yourself.
4. Don't violate your own morals.
5. Control your emotions.
6. Increase your knowledge.
7. Seek a relationship with God.
8. Be responsible.
9. Respect others.
10. Be quick to forgive others.
11. Be friendly to everyone you meet.
12. Give sincere encouragement to people.
13. Don't lie.
14. Make good decisions.

"If you never ask, the answer is always no" ~ Nora Roberts

When we are afraid of trying new things, we will slip right back into our comfort zone. Knowledge, and the confidence to use the knowledge we acquire, will keep us from getting in our own way. Don't let "what-iffing" immobilize you. People don't resist change— they resist being changed!

Don't make excuses. You are just getting in the way of achieving your dreams. Always aim for the greatest achievements you can imagine and go for it! YOU are in charge. YOU are a powerful and successful person.

Suffering In Silence

"Attitude determines altitude." ~ Dr. Karackas Watkins

"No one can make you feel inferior without your consent."
~ Eleanor Roosevelt

You wouldn't worry about what others think of you if you stopped to realize how little they do think of you! My dad lived his life around the "what will people think" concept. As long as you aren't doing anything wrong or hurting others, you shouldn't live your life around other people's thoughts and opinions.

Are you a product of circumstances? John Maxwell stated, "I am not a product of my circumstances. I am a product of my decisions." We can only make decisions with the information we have at the time the decision is being made. Often, we gain additional information after the decision is made and we may be forced to adjust our previous decision. It's okay to change your mind! You now have additional information with additional facts to make a more accurate determination. This is all part of life and it's okay to make changes.

"Make the best use of what is in your power and
take the rest as it happens." ~ Epictetus

We need to take control of our lives! Have you noticed how many people always have the answers to your problems but not their own problems? It is always easier to see out than to see in. Don't allow yourself to become a victim. Suck it up, saddle up, and take total control of your journey through life.

"You cannot escape the responsibility of tomorrow
by evading it today." ~ Abraham Lincoln

Not taking responsibility may be less demanding, less painful, and mean less time spent in the unknown. It's certainly more comfortable. You can just take it easy and blame problems in your life on someone else. But there is always a price to pay. When you don't take responsibility for your life, you give away your personal power, your dreams, and your self-identity.

Often we stand in our own way and in the way of our success. Our thoughts become our actions. If we don't take responsibility for our lives, those thoughts stay on our mental stage and go nowhere. Taking responsibility for our life is that extra ingredient that makes taking action more of a natural thing. Don't get stuck in the thinking and wishing mode.

Thoughts + Actions = Results

Thoughts and plans are always great, but without action you will never get results! You must have all three to move forward and succeed.

Sometimes the best decision we can make is to be quiet. We have nothing to prove. We're not trying to convince anyone that we are great people. We're not trying to fix what we didn't break. We're not fighting for anyone to see our worth. Whatever someone else does is on them. As for us, we need to move forward, free and at peace.

You never really know the true impact you have on those around you. You never know how much someone needed that smile you gave them. You never know how much your kindness turned someone's entire life around. You never know how much someone needed that long hug or deep talk. So don't wait to be kind. Don't wait for someone else to be kind first. Don't wait for better circumstances or for someone to change. Just be kind, because you never know how much someone needs it.

Ladies, when another woman talks badly about you for no reason at all, don't be quick to strike back. Pray for that woman! She sees something in you that she doesn't see in herself. Remember, confidence is silent and insecurity is loud.

A satisfied life is better than a successful life, because our success is measured by others, but our satisfaction is measured by our own soul, mind, and heart. Peace of mind is worth a lot!

God Has a Purpose

If God is making you wait, there is a purpose.

If God is making you persevere, there is a purpose.

If God is making you surrender, there is a purpose.

If God is making you adapt, there is a purpose.

If God is making you reflect, there is a purpose.

If God is making you overcome, there is a purpose.

Blessed are those who trust in God, for they will receive more than they ever prayed for. Amen!

"Life's best chapters are written after the hardest battles.
Keep going. God gives his toughest battles to his strongest soldiers."
~ Joanne Kanute

Self-worth is the belief that your life has value and significance. Low self-worth can result from how you see or perceive yourself and how you think others see or perceive you. Faulty perceptions lead to faulty conclusions. Today's society has people thinking their self-worth is based on money, possessions, education, or beauty. When we use a value system as a measuring tool for self-worth, it couldn't make conclusions further from the truth.

"You are the one in control of how much energy you give away!"
~ Andrew Carnegie

What can I change so I can move forward?

**If you fully believed in yourself,
what would you do differently?**

Do not let your hearts be troubled. Trust in God; trust also in me.
(John 14:1 TLV)

*They will have no fear of bad news; their hearts are steadfast,
trusting in the Lord.* (Psalms 112:7 NIV)

*"But they all alike began to make excuses. The first said, 'I have just
bought a field, and I must go and see it. Please excuse me.'"*
(Luke 14: 18 NIV)

Clear the clutter

*"Clutter is not just stuff on the floor, but anything that stands
between you and the life you wish to be living."* ~ Peter Walsh

One day you will realize that material things mean nothing. All that matters is the well-being of the people in your life and your eternal destination. Don't complicate life. We won't be here forever and life is short. Your time is too valuable to waste on nonsense. Decluttering is about removing the things we don't want or need. Minimalism is about discovering how little we actually need.

Here are a few starting steps to clear your clutter:

1. **Stuff you don't use anymore.**
   Are you holding onto things you don't use? Look around your office, home, and car. What could you give away (if it's in good condition) or throw away (because it's broken or in bad shape)? Many people hold on to things out of fear that they will need them in the future. At that point in time, the question is, will you be able to find it? Be willing to let go of things when you no longer need them or use them.

2. **Projects you are procrastinating on.**
   You may not think of it as clutter, but that old to-do list that keeps rolling over in your head every day is clutter for your brain. Either drop the projects, complete them now, or give yourself a new and reasonable deadline.

3. **Too much stuff in too little space.**
   If you are one of the many who crams everything into an undersized space, it's time to make room in your environment. From your desk at work to your bathroom counters, overcrowding your physical space can leave you feeling mentally overcrowded. Psychologically speaking, when you make space in your environment, you make room for more of what you want in your life.

4. **Mess, junk, and stuff that is in disarray!**

   When things are completely out of order, it is more difficult to plan, strategize, think, or take action effectively. Before ending your day, take five minutes to put things in order—at work, home and in your car—so that you can start fresh the next day.

5. **Things you don't like.**

   Is there anything in your car, home, or office that you simply don't like? Your various environments should inspire you, not depress, frustrate, or irritate you. Make sure your different environments are filled with the sights, scents, and sounds you love most.

KISS = Keep It Simple and Sophisticated

Simple doesn't mean easy! Some of the simplest things are often the hardest to accomplish. Not everything will ever go your way, so don't expect too much. It's easy to criticize but much harder to realize the reason why you're criticizing. Is it possible it's out of jealousy or perhaps boredom?

Live in the moment and be aware of everything you're doing, feeling, and telling yourself. Be kind to the people around you. If no one likes you, you probably won't get too far in life. If you don't like what is being said, change the conversation. Ask yourself why you do the things you do. If you have trouble coming up with a meaningful answer, then chances are you shouldn't do it.

Redefine what success means to you; redefine what life means to you. And **STOP** focusing and worrying about how other people live their lives! Life is joyfully simple. Let's keep it that way.

We live in a culture where people continuously strive for more—more of everything. They want to be more, do more, have more. The message is "more is better." Having more doesn't increase your worth as a human being. More often than not, **less is MORE**! The more we have in our lives, the more time it requires to maintain that life.

You can design the life you want to live. You can design a simple life, a life with purpose. Ask yourself these simple questions:

Who are you?

What is your purpose in life?

What are you meant to do or be?

"Simplicity is the ultimate Sophistication." ~ Leonardo da Vinci

Organization is a vital key to a successful lifestyle. Getting yourself organized will give a greater confidence in yourself. Plus you will send out a stronger self-image. Getting your life organized at home and work will help relieve some of the stress in your life.

Just because someone asks you to do something, that does not oblige you to do it. Practice graciously saying NO. Your time is valuable, and gaining control of it is a critical aspect of moving close to where you want to be in life.

Keep your workspace clutter free; concentrate on one thing at a time. Here are some helpful tips:

Get organized:

    a.   Get a planner

    b.   Be willing to make serious changes

    c.   Identify your true priorities

    d.   Notice how you spend your time

    e.   Drop or modify activities that are not top priorities

    f.   Plan your schedule six to twelve months in advance

    g.   Learn to anticipate potential bumps in the road and resolve them before they become major obstacles

12 Benefits of Being Well Organized:

1. You will be able to be more focused on what you want to achieve.
2. You will be able to be more productive.
3. You will be able to manage your time more effectively.
4. You will be able to do your work more economically.
5. You will be able to reduce the clutter in your workspace and reduce your stress levels.
6. You will be able to achieve more balance in your life.
7. You will be able to set and achieve your goals in a more efficient manner.
8. You will be able to present a more positive business image.
9. You will be able to prioritize your tasks.
10. You will be able to be more flexible and more creative.
11. You will be able to achieve more energy and enthusiasm.
12. You will be able to achieve freedom from chaos.

Declutter:

- **Don't keep gifts out of guilt** – it's okay to donate an item and not feel guilty.
- **Rid yourself of miscellaneous items** – spare buttons, unidentified cords, free novelty items, etc. Clear them out!
- **Storage experts are hoarders** – sort before you store!
- **One year rule** – if you haven't used an item or worn it, get it out of the house.
- **Broken beyond repair** – it needs to be gone!
- **Not even yours** – give it back to the person who owns it.
- **"Just in case…"** – think very carefully about these items. Maybe they don't matter now.
- **Publications** – it is easier to find articles, etc. on the internet now than look through a bunch of publications you're saving.

**What beliefs or patterns are fueling
the accumulation of clutter?**

What is the impact of clutter on your overall well-being?

What are your specific goals for decluttering?

"Do not store up for yourselves treasures on earth, where moth and rust destroy, and where thieves break in and steal. But store up for yourselves treasures in heaven, where neither moth nor rust destroys and where thieves do not break in and steal. For where your treasure is, there your heart will be also." (Matthew 6: 19-21 TLV)

Goal Setting With Purpose

"A Goal is a dream with a deadline." ~ Napoleon Hill

"The purpose of life is a life of purpose." ~ Robert Byrne

"Life is a journey that must be traveled no matter how bad the roads and accommodations." ~ Oliver Goldsmith

Everyone needs a purpose to their life! The definition of purpose is: "the reason for which something is done, created, or for which something exists." When you set goals, something inside of you starts saying, "Let's go! Let's go!" and ceilings start to move.

"Success doesn't knock on your door; you have to build it from the ground up." ~ Milton Berle

SMART GOALS:

> S - Specific
> M - Measurable
> A - Attainable
> R - Relevant
> T - Time-bound

"Your life has purpose, your story is important, your dreams count, your voice matters, you were born to make an impact!"
~ Author Unknown

Purpose – everyone one of us needs a purpose to our life. Without purpose we have no goals, and without goals, we have no destination or drive. When one loses PURPOSE to live, it will ultimately lead to destruction. Instead of going through life without any meaning or purpose, begin doing things because you want to do them, not because you have to. Here are a few thoughts:

- **Be happy** – happy is a choice; it comes from the inside out. You can learn to be happy each day by simply being grateful!
- **Show up** – are you letting life just happen or are you creating life and taking action on the things that will make your life the way you want it to be?
- **Follow your heart** – do what you love to do and do it often!
- **Find a new perspective** – take the frame away from what you see and change the perspective.
- **Have a sense of wonder** – children are the classic example of "wonder" about everything. They ask lots of questions and want to know why!
- **Find people you love** – people you look up to, people with whom you share the same passions, ideas, and hobbies.
- **Set goals** – Remember Winston Churchill said, "He who fails to plan, plans to fail."
- **Help others** – do for others what you want for yourself. Helping others will give you a feeling of satisfaction and worthiness.
- **Dance – often**!!
- **Pamper yourself** – you will be glad you did.
- **Face your fears** – just do it already!! One way to overcome something is to do it!
- **Go to a museum** – get out and do something; learn something new!

- **Exercise** – exercise releases endorphins, "happy hormones" that reduce stress. Exercise is a way to keep fit and healthy, lengthening your life span.
- **Limit television** – find something else to do. Read a book, play a game—get creative.
- **Enjoy natur**e – take a walk, go to the park, listen to the birds, or look at the flowers.

If you don't know where you're going, how will you know when you get there? Have a clear picture in your mind of what you want; visualize it down to the smallest detail. Be sure to write your goals down. Goals that are written down will not be forgotten.

Commit yourself to this picture and its realization and make it part of your everyday life. Then enjoy it when it appears. Living is a thing you do NOW, not tomorrow, not next week, not next month, not next year or never.

Form an action plan to accomplish all your goals:

Action Plan:

- Exactly what are you going to do?
- How much will you do?
- When will you do it?
- How often will you do it?

Four Mistakes to avoid as you set your new goals:

- Aiming at too much
- Not aiming at all

- Aiming at the past
- Keeping your goals to yourself

Tips to setting goals:

- Determine if the goal is maintenance or progress
- Determine if the goal is urgent or important
- Get the environment right
- Get the timing right
- Avoid postponing important tasks
- Spend time planning and organizing
- Prioritize
- Use a to-do list
- Be flexible
- Do the right thing properly
- Avoid being a perfectionist
- Conquer procrastination

"Time is free, but it's priceless. You can't own it, but you can use it. You can't keep it, but you can spend it. Once you've lost it you can never get it back." ~ Henry Mac Kay

"You are never too old to set another goal or to dream a new dream." ~ C.S. Lewis

Valorie Burton advised there were four mistakes to avoid as you set your new goals. These suggestions came from her Week 2, 2009 Newsletter:

1. **Aiming at too much.**
   Sure, you may have a long list of bad habits you'd like to break, but if you resolve to break them all at once, you're likely to overwhelm yourself and give up. Instead, build your confidence by setting small goals that you can reach in the near term. **Make your goals small, specific and attainable.**

2. **Not aiming at all.**
   Worse than aiming too high is having no vision for where you are headed. **Goals contribute to happiness and well-being.** They don't have to be daunting or terribly serious. Create "fun goals" centered around activities that bring you joy and lots of positive emotion. Perhaps it's a hobby you commit to engaging in at least once a week or something you add to your schedule that you can look forward to daily.

3. **Aiming at the past.**
   People often feel pressured to "catch up" on all the things they think they should have done last year or the year before, so they pile on resolutions out of anxiety over missed opportunities and procrastination. Can you relate? **Forgive yourself for what you didn't do in the past and focus on the present. It's the only moment you can do anything about.**

4. **Keeping your goals to yourself.**
   Research shows that when you **publicly declare a goal**, you are **more likely to achieve it**. It is an act of commitment that makes it more real. And the accountability of telling someone else your intentions is a

motivator. When you keep your goals a secret, it's too easy to let yourself off the hook!

So share your goals with those who will encourage you along the way and whose opinion you value.

5. **Keep on keeping on** – there are many days we don't have the drive to keep pressing on, but one must keep on keeping on even if you don't find the need.

Keep Trying! Keep Reaching! Keep Dreaming!

Nothing beautiful ever came from an easy life. Nothing truly incredible ever came from times of simplicity and contentment. We naturally want to reach for more. Don't wait until you reach your goal to be proud of yourself. Be proud of yourself every step of the way. Celebrate small wins. Success is a series of steps, not just one big leap.

"When obstacles arise, you change your direction to reach your goal; you don't change your decision to get there." ~ Zig Ziglar

Don't let people who are not going anywhere take you with them. Allow yourself to embrace the journey of life, and enjoy the moment at each stage as you'll never be back there again. Nothing remains for too long, not even our sorrows.

Many days you will wonder if anyone cares or even notices you. As a rule of thumb, you are always more loved than you think you are. And people are always watching whether they say anything or not. The pointless days will add up to something in the end. Anything worth having is worth waiting for.

The only thing that is standing in the way of your own happiness is you. If you want to change, you must make the change. Acting on it is crucial. At no time were you told or taught that you would live in a magnificent land of beauty and happiness every day, and if you were, it was a lie.

It's never the circumstances that drive us to madness; it's always how we think about them. Sometimes you will have to try a thousand times before you succeed. We live in a world of information overload and tend to get caught up in over thinking everything.

"There are better things ahead than any we leave behind."
~ C.S. Lewis

It is always better to be someone who tried and failed as opposed to someone who was too weak to try at all. If you're genuinely unhappy, there's only one thing you must do to change everything—think differently!!

The first steps are always the hardest. Take the first step and begin your journey of life. Take baby steps if that's what you need to do. Take one step at a time, but start!! Putting your goals in writing can help you make your dreams a reality.

"Without God, life has no purpose, and without purpose, life has no meaning. Without meaning, life has no significance or hope."
~ Rick Warren

Do you know your purpose in life?

What are your goals and do you have them in writing?

Suffering In Silence

Many are the plans in a person's heart, but it is the Lord's purpose that prevails. (Proverbs 19:21 NIV)

For I know the plans I have for you," declares the LORD, "plans to prosper you and not to harm you, plans to give you hope and a future. (Jeremiah 29:11 NIV)

9
Build Your Team

Same Direction & Destination

"Coming together is a beginning. Keeping together is progress. Working together is success." ~ Henry Ford

Surround yourself with people who have the same goals and interest; talk about business, saving money, and living better. Make sure your circle motivates and inspires you to do better. It's not the size of your circle that matters, but the loyalty of those within it. Teamwork is not just for sports or careers; you need a strong team to do life with. I don't know who needs to hear this but losing people who treat you poorly isn't actually a loss.

"Your journey is not the same as mine, and my journey is not yours, but if we meet on a certain path, may we encourage each other."
~ Unknown

Surround yourself with people who want to see you win.

No drama.

No jealousy.

No hidden agendas.

Just genuine support, real love, and pure intentions. Most people don't want to be part of the process; they just want to be part of the outcome. But the process is where you figure out who's worth being part of the outcome. Sometimes it's a difference of opinion and sometimes it's a difference of morals.

Teamwork Quotes:

- Alone we can do so little; together we can do so much.
  ~ Helen Keller
- None of us is as smart as all of us. *~ Kenneth Blanchard*
- It takes two flints to make a fire. *~ Louisa May Alcott*
- The value of achievement lies in the achieving.
  ~ Albert Einstein
- If you want to lift yourself up, lift up someone else.
  ~ Booker T Washington
- Teamwork makes the dream work. *~ John Maxwell*

What are the 5 Cs of teamwork?

The five Cs of teamwork are communication, camaraderie, commitment, confidence, and coach-ability. These elements are interdependent and contribute to a team's success:

- **Communication:** Effective communication is a key component of teamwork.
- **Camaraderie:** A sense of camaraderie can help build a strong team.
- **Commitment:** Team members should be dedicated to the team's goals and be willing to put in the effort to achieve them.

- **Confidence:** Confidence can help a team perform well.
- **Coachability:** A team that is coachable can learn and grow together.

Organizations can promote these principles to enhance teamwork, drive innovation, and achieve their goals.

Here are six key steps to building and maintaining a strong and effective team:

1. **Define the purpose**

   Providing a clear, inspiring vision sets the foundation for successful teamwork and helps guide the direction of the group when they face challenges and decisions.

2. **Assemble the team**

   All team members should trust, respect and support each other. Select members with complementary skills and abilities who can bring a diverse range of viewpoints and ideas to the table.

3. **Determine the goals**

   Decide the role that each team member will play. Be sure to also consider other resources required in terms of time, materials, space, support, and money.

4. **Set expectations**

   Setting clear standards from the outset will ensure that each member's conduct and contributions are appropriate.

5. **Monitor and review**

   Monitoring and reviewing progress allow for adjustments and improvements to be incorporated along the way.

6. Celebrate and reward

Ensure that recognition is consistent and that the method you choose inspires and reinforces the team members to continue their positive contribution to the team's progress.

Here's something we can all agree on: we want our lives to matter. We all want to live a satisfying, fulfilling, and purposeful life. I don't believe this is just a selfish desire but a need for a purposeful life. Feeling a certain amount of significance in your life is healthy.

Building Your Strong Team

Part I: The Mission

Every team has a mission that it strives to accomplish. Thinking about your life as a team sport forces you to realize an important lesson: your life is dramatically impacted by the people around you. Life is a shared experience. And for this reason, the people around you need to be part of the plan. A good mission in life is always about more than just you.

Part II: The Coaches

Great teams have a coach who aligns with their mission. It's important to have the right type of person to lead the team.

Just like in sports, there are coaches—or mentors—in our lives. In one way or another, you are an apprentice of your parents, your professors, your boss, and so on. They coach you towards certain habits, they teach you how to approach problems in life, and they impact what you believe about the world. Much of what you believe and how you act is determined by these people. The people around us guide our behaviors in one way or another, whether it's good or bad!

Part III: The Captain

Good teams always have a captain. They need someone who can carry the banner and set the tone for the rest of the group.

Part IV: The Teammates

Great teams have players who want greatness. Great teams are filled with people who want the same things. There are people around you who will also believe in your mission. These people are your teammates. They connect with your values and share your priorities. I like thinking about life as a team sport!

Part V: Team Health

- **Trust and Honesty:** Are you comfortable and willing to be yourself and share ideas through healthy discussion and debate?
- **Collaboration:** Are you able to work together as a team to identify obstacles and solve them together?
- **Accountability:** Do you hold one another to commitments? Are you willing to admit when mistakes are made or where improvement is necessary?
- **Idea Meritocracy:** Does everyone have a seat and a voice at the table? How are solutions to the problems explored?
- **Feedback and Growth:** Are you open to receiving and sharing feedback, as well as exploring innovative ways to solve problems or simply improve?

Every detour in life becomes a chance to learn, evolve, and discover some new strength. You come to realize that the quality of people you hang out with matters more than the quantity.

"Everybody has a home team: it's the people you call when you get a flat tire or when something terrible happens. It's people who, near or far, know everything that's wrong with you and love you anyways. These are the ones who tell you their secrets, who get themselves a glass of water without asking when they're at your house. These are the people who cry when you cry. These are your people, your middle-of-the-night, no-matter-what people." ~ Author Unknown

Common Traits

"The secret, Alice is to surround yourself with people who make your heart smile. It's then, only then, that you'll find Wonderland." ~ Lewis Carroll

You can't change others, but you can set limits that change how they show up in your life. Finding people with the same common traits is important because it fosters strong fulfilling relationships and can positively impact your well-being. Shared interests, values, and personality traits can lead to easier communication, deeper communication, and mutual support. These types of connections can offer more opportunities for learning, growth, and a sense of belonging.

Here are a few reasons why finding people with shared traits are of benefit:

- Easier communication
- Stronger relationships
- Mutual support and understanding
- Increased happiness and well-being
- Personal growth and learning
- Shared experiences and activities

As we journey through life, you will come into contact with many different people who you connect with for various reasons and purposes. It could be a project, church activities, school connections, parenting connections, job, volunteering, etc. We make contact with people in many different ways and through those contacts we often find our people!

Common traits are what form friendships and friendships can have a big impact on your health and well-being. However, people we connect with for various reasons that we don't share common traits with can impact our health in a negative way as well. Learn to deal with those you have nothing in common with, but realize a lasting friendship may never develop.

**What are some of the common traits
you value in a friendship?**

**What are some of the steps you can take to create
more positive and fulfilling relationships?**

Support and Trust

A wise man once said, "Be careful who you let on your ship, because some people will sink the whole ship because they can't be the captain." ~ Eleanor Johnson

It's not the size of your circle that matters, but the loyalty of those within it. Having a support system is so important. Remember to always surround yourself with people who genuinely care for you, support you, and want the best for you. There's something so beautiful about having long-term friends that have witnessed multiple versions of you and loved you unconditionally through it all.

There isn't a single person on the entire planet who is entitled to treat you badly, hurt you, or make you feel badly about yourself, and then avoid you. Remember that. We will meet many different types of people throughout our lives, but they won't all become your friends.

Often friends and family won't encourage you to try anything new, and you'll wind up staying exactly where you are—complacent, unhappy, dissatisfied or unsatisfied, and wishing you could move forward with your life.

The term "too busy" is a myth. People make time for the things that are important to them. Don't focus on who let you down—appreciate who was there to lift you up. So often we hear or find ourselves saying, "I was too busy" or "I'm so busy." More often than not, this is a way to excuse ourselves from something we don't value enough to take the time to do. It's all about **priority**! Everyone's lives are busy but stop and think about how many hours you spend every day looking at an electronic screen or watching something on your television. Are you really too busy to help a friend, volunteer at your church, or connect with a family member to see how they are doing?

Not only do we need other people, but we also need to be available for others as well. A life team may be exactly what is needed to maintain priorities.

A "Life Team" refers to a small group of people who actively support and encourage each other in their personal growth and development across different areas of life. These areas include relationships, careers, health, and spirituality. This team essentially acts as a network of trusted individuals who walk alongside you through life's challenges and milestones, often emphasizing shared values and a commitment to mutual accountability. Most people don't want to be part of the process; they just want to be part of the outcome. But the process is where you figure out who's worth being part of the outcome.

Key points about a Life Team:

- **Purpose:**
  To provide support, guidance, and encouragement for personal growth and development.
- **Composition:**
  A small group of individuals with shared values who can offer different perspectives and expertise.
- **Functioning:**
  Regular meetings, open communication, and a focus on accountability to help each member achieve their goals.

Where you might hear the term Life Team:

- **Church communities:**

Some churches utilize Life Teams as a group of members dedicated to supporting others in their spiritual journey.

- **Personal development:**
Life coaches or individuals seeking significant personal growth often assemble a Life Team of trusted advisors.

Aspects of Building Trust and Support with your Team:

- **Open communication:** share goals, listen to the feedback and concerns of your team members
- **Empowerment:** trust you team members to help make decisions
- **Positive feedback:** appreciate individual achievements and how it contributes to the team
- **Mentorship:** be open to learning and developing new skills from your team members
- **Work-life balance:** respect personal time and a healthy work-life balance for your team members
- **Engagement:** people tend to be more motivated and engaged if they feel trusted and supported
- **Conflict resolution:** address disagreements constructively – everyone wants to be heard
- **Reduce stress:** when the team supports each other, they feel less stress and burnout
- **Improved productivity:** a strong team will always be more productive

What is so important about our shared values, vision, mission, etc.?

What strengths do you bring to your life team?

10
Power of Positive Self-Image and Self-Esteem

"Low self-esteem is like driving through life with your hand-break on." ~ Maxwell Maltz

"One of the greatest regrets in life is being what others would want you to be, rather than being yourself." ~ Shannon Alder

"You are what you are and where you are because of what's gone into your mind. You can change what you are and where you are by changing what goes into your mind." ~ Zig Ziglar

"A positive mind finds opportunity in everything. A negative mind finds fault in everything." ~ Dhande Sir

What is Self-Image and Self-Esteem?

What exactly is self-image?

A simple definition of a person's self-image is their answer to this question, "What do you believe people think about you?" Now that doesn't mean this is really what they think about you, but rather what

YOU think they are thinking! And what you think is what matters and what we must take action to change.

What God knows about you is more important than what others think about you. God knows your heart and created you in His image.

We all have many people who influence our lives, but we ultimately MUST be the ones to take charge of our own lives. Stop being a slave to your mind and start deciding how you want to live. As a rule of thumb, you are always more loved than you think you are. There will be days that seem pointless, but those pointless days will add up to something in the end. Anything worth having is worth waiting and fighting for.

The only thing withholding you from your own happiness is YOU. If you want change in your life, then change! Acting on it is crucial. You were never ever told or taught that you would live in a magnificent land of beauty and happiness every day. And if you were told that, it shouldn't take long to realize it's a fairy tale and not the real world.

It's not the circumstances that drive us to madness; it's always our opinion of the circumstances. Many times, you will have to try over and over again before you succeed. It's your life—make it an interesting story!

> *"There are better things ahead than any we leave behind."*
> ~ C.S. Lewis

People that take charge of their lives and mold them into the type of lifestyle they want don't get affected by what people tell them. Instead, they listen to their inner gut and go by what feels right for them. We can learn from other people but ultimately, we need to take responsibility for our own actions and decisions.

Successful people choose to do what they want to do rather than what they think they have to do. If you want to begin to really take charge of your life and direct it in the right way so that you can build a lifestyle many would die for, you must learn to take responsibility for everything—the good, the bad, and the ugly! Your life is yours to live, no one else's. Choose what you want and go for it. We only go around once, so make it count.

We all have many people who influence our lives, but we ultimately MUST take charge of our own life! Stop being a slave to your mind and start deciding how you want to live!

People can destroy your image, damage your personality, and create rumors about you, but they can never take away your good deeds or good intentions. No matter how they choose to describe you, twisting narratives to fit their own agendas, you will always be held in high regard by those who truly know you best.

"No one can make you feel inferior without your consent."
~ Eleanor Roosevelt

Allow yourself to embrace the journey of life. Sometimes we need to pause and enjoy the moment, as we'll never be at that place in our lives again. Nothing remains for too long, not even our sorrows. Just because we carry it well doesn't mean it's not heavy.

Statistics have found that lack of self-esteem can actually extinguish some people's desire to go on living. James Dobson said, "If I could write a prescription for the women of the world, I would provide each of them with a healthy dose of self-esteem and personal worth...I have no doubt that this is their greatest need."

There are five key ingredients to living a life of fulfillment which gives us greater self-esteem:

- **Faith** – you have to believe in something. God put you here for a reason!
- **Direction** – you must have direction if you are going to accomplish anything worthwhile.
- **Consistent Action and Purpose** – you can only reach your goals by taking consistent action. Being consistent means setting aside time to accomplish your goals. Consistent action includes taking care of yourself. You will function more efficiently if your mind and body are functioning at peak conditions. Everyone needs a purpose to their life.
- **Flexibility** – don't fear change! Changes become necessary when you obtain information that wasn't previously available when you made your original decision.
- **Patience** – without patience you will never reach your destination. You will give up in frustration.

What is self-acceptance: the ability to love yourself unconditionally, no matter what flaws and traits exist:

- **Set intent** – stand on the positive, forget the negative.
- **Rejoice in your strengths** – make a list of your strengths and hold onto them.

- **Consider the people you surround yourself with –** surround yourself with positive people.
- **Form a support system** – distance yourself from people who bring you down.
- **Forgive yourself** – we all have made errors through life. Life is a learning process! Forgive yourself and move forward.
- **Fake it until you make it!**

What is self-esteem: self-esteem is how we value ourselves. It is how we perceive our value to the world and how valuable we think we are to others. Self-esteem affects our trust in others, our relationships, and our work—nearly every part of our lives. Positive self-esteem gives us strength and flexibility to take charge of our lives and grow from our mistakes without the fear of rejection.

Four of the deadliest ways to bring defeat and failure to your life:

1. **Low self-esteem paralyzes your potential** – it seems we all have to struggle against this; however, some struggle far greater than others. Low self-esteem is often referred to as a fog and some days it is thicker than others.
2. **Low self-esteem destroys your dreams** – with the wrong kind of vision about yourself, by undervaluing yourself as inferior and unable, you will surely self-destruct.
3. **Low self-esteem ruins your relationships** – when you have a proper and healthy opinion of yourself then you are able to give to others.

4. **Low self-esteem sabotages your Christian service –** you don't give God a chance to show his power and ability through your weakness.

According to Dr. Maurice Wagner, a professional Christian counselor, there are three essential components of a **healthy self-image**:

1. **A sense of belonging, of being loved.** This is simply awareness of being wanted, accepted, cared for, enjoyed, and loved.
2. **A sense of worth and value.** "I count. I am valued. I have something to offer."
3. **A sense of being competent.** "I can do this task. I can cope with that situation. I am able to meet life."

Have you ever struggled with keeping a positive self-image, self-esteem, or self-confidence?

Twelve reasons why self-esteem is important:

1. You believe you are worthy of happiness; you feel worthy of respect.
2. It's the first step in believing in you and it builds self-confidence. If you do not respect yourself, do you think that others will?
3. Your self-esteem has a profound effect on your thinking, emotions, happiness, desires, values, and goals.
4. You can still feel respect and be proud even if you make a mistake.

5. You never compare yourself to others and your self-confidence is strong.
6. You have a sense of control and direction. You approach problems with a different perspective. This allows you to make correct choices and be proud of the actions you take.
7. It allows you to act independently and to assume responsibility for you actions, goals, and desires.
8. You become empowered to take new challenges and handle criticism.
9. You consider yourself a valuable person and you live for a reason.
10. It gives the clarity needed to recognize your qualities. It provides strong faith in yourself and lets you know that you are lovable and capable.
11. It is an integral part of personal happiness, fulfilling relationships, and the achievement of your desires.
12. It allows you to be in control of your own life and able to do what you want to do. It is the source of your mental health.

That's Why It's So Important!!!

Low self-esteem is a debilitating condition that keeps individuals from realizing their full potential. A person with low self-esteem often will feel unworthy, incapable, and incompetent.

Developing good self-esteem involves encouraging a positive (but realistic) attitude toward yourself and the world around you and appreciating your worth, while at the same time behaving responsibly toward others. Self-esteem isn't self-absorption; it's self-respect!

Outward signs of positive self-esteem:

1. Confidence
2. Self-direction
3. Non-blaming behavior
4. An awareness of personal strengths
5. Ability to make mistakes and learn from them
6. Ability to accept mistakes from others
7. Optimism
8. Ability to solve problems
9. Independent and cooperative attitude
10. Feeling comfortable with a wide range of emotions
11. Ability to trust others
12. A good sense of personal limitations
13. Good self-care
14. Ability to say NO

Signs of low self-esteem:

1. Negative view of life
2. Perfectionist attitude
3. Mistrusting others – even those who show signs of affection
4. Blaming behavior
5. Fear of taking risks
6. Feelings of being unloved and unlovable
7. Dependence – letting others make decisions
8. Fear of being ridiculed

What people see on the outside lets them know how you feel on the inside. Perhaps no issue is more important to emotional well-being than our sense of self.

The relationship you have with your body image influences your self-esteem and confidence. No one has a perfect body image. Even those we think do...don't! We all have many people who influence our lives, but we ultimately MUST take charge of our life and thoughts! Stop being a slave to your mind and start deciding how you want to live! Self-acceptance is about recognizing that you are a process, not a product.

- **Express yourself** – we should never feel bad about expressing ourselves, and don't ever apologize by doing so! However, the way we do so should remain very tactful. Everyone has the right to express their opinion.
- **Say "NO"** – saying NO is not a bad thing!! We always allow ourselves to feel badly when we have to tell someone no, but saying no to a situation or circumstance means saying YES to something else.

5 Steps to Saying "No"

- Figure out what you really want.
- Find the "YES" – most of the times when you say "no" to something, you are saying YES to something else.
- Don't babble – you don't need excuses or to project a meek, nervous, or uncertain attitude.
- Offer what you can – be honest with them about what you can accomplish.
- Move on – no dwelling, fretting, or second-guessing.

"Overthinking is the biggest cause of our unhappiness; keep yourself occupied. Keep your mind off things that don't help you. Think positive." ~ Simple Reminders

What builds our self-image?

Appearance – there are a number of factors which impact our appearance, and when they all come together, our appearance is formed. The main factors which impact our image are: balance of appearance, facial shape, hairstyle, skin tone, fashion personality, personality type, grooming, tone of voice, facial expression, eye contact, gestures, body language, and etiquette.

A first impression is formed within 7 seconds. You will never be given a second chance to make a good FIRST IMPRESSION! Seven out of ten Americans say physical appearance is important "in terms of happiness, social life, and the ability to get ahead." Looking good on the outside is what makes people want to look inside to see what you are all about. The outside shell is the packaging of what lies within. Looking your best makes you feel good and when you feel good, you can accomplish more!

"Looking your best strengthens your self-image; a stronger self-image increases your self-esteem; and a greater self-esteem brings greater SUCCESS!" ~ Joanne Kanute

Brian Tracy, author of *The Psychology of Achievement*, stated "Many capable men and women are disqualified from job opportunities because they simply do not look the part."

What exactly does your appearance say about you?

1. **Self-esteem:** what people see on the outside lets them know how you feel on the inside.

2. **Self-respect:** those who respect themselves dress accordingly.
3. **Confidence:** your goal is to create an appearance of confidence when you walk in the room.
4. **Organizational skills:** recruiters often say they use appearance to judge organizational skills.
5. **Attention to detail:** 90 percent of your image is made by clothing.
6. **Creativity:** accessories show your creativity.
7. **Soundness of judgment:** understanding and wearing the appropriate outfit shows accurate decision making.
8. **Reliability:** all of the above factors form the big picture down to the details.

None of this means you need to rush out and buy yourself a new expensive wardrobe, but we need to be mindful of how we look and maximize our existing wardrobe!

Seven rules to life:

1. Let it go
2. Ignore them
3. Give it time
4. Don't compare
5. Stay calm
6. It's on you
7. Always smile

"Some of us never found time to be happy because we were too busy trying to be strong." ~ Author Unknown

Never regret being a good person to the wrong people. Your behavior says everything about you; their behavior says enough about them.

"Self-honesty is the only way of avoidance. You must lean into the pain you've been avoiding and the life you have created. This is how you rise again." ~ J. Mike Fields

Traits that build a stronger social image:

- Powerful Listening
- Feel Empathetically
- Respond Carefully
- Act Authentically
- Acknowledge Generously

Setbacks are an important part of life. Instead of thinking of a setback in a negative way, think of it as a life-learning experience. Sometimes it takes a setback to make us see that some of our habits are not productive and it's time to make some changes. Setbacks will only make you stronger!

Let me tell you, people can be very cruel. And sometimes those people are family. I'll never forget the time my great aunt and uncle were visiting from Seattle; I hadn't seen them since I was a little girl. My father introduced me to them, saying: "This is our daughter, Joanne, and she is our fat one." I absolutely wanted to crawl under the carpet I was standing on. To add more salt to the wound, I was at work and all of my co-workers heard the introduction.

At that moment I made the decision that he would not introduce me to any more family members as "the fat one." I made that statement my motivation rather than dwelling on it and becoming depressed. (I lost 92 ½ pounds, and yes, I struggle every day with my weight!)

Don't get caught up in the "drama" world we seem to live in these days. There seems to be more people who feed on "drama" than ever before. DON'T GO THERE! Drama doesn't produce anything positive.

Tips for living with Self-Doubt:

1. **Live in the present** – most of the time self-doubt comes from memories of the past.
2. **Trust in yourself** – we can be our own worst enemy.
3. **Find the source of your self-doubt** – once you find the source of your problem and understand it, you can begin to fix it.
4. **Spend time with others** – too much alone time can make you overthink your problems.

What are some of the things you struggle with about self-image and self-esteem?

What are some of the ways you feel you could improve in this area of your life?

There is therefore now no condemnation to those who are in Christ Jesus, who do not walk according to the flesh, but according to the Spirit. For the law of the Spirit of life in Christ Jesus has made me free from the law of sin and death. (Romans 8:1-2 NKJV)

"Before I formed you in the womb I knew you; before you were born I sanctified you; I ordained you a prophet to the nations."
(Jeremiah 1:5 NKJV)

For we are God's handiwork, created in Christ Jesus to do good works, which God prepared in advance for us to do.
(Ephesians 2:10 NIV)

Self-Care

"Almost everything will work again if you unplug it for a few minutes – including you." ~ Anne Lamott

"Self-care means giving yourself permission to pause." ~ Cecilia Tran

"You can't pour from an empty cup; take care of yourself first."
~ Adam Grant

Take care of yourself because burnout can sneak up on you! Burning the candle at both ends will catch up to you in a number of ways. If you are unhealthy, it becomes very difficult to accomplish much.

Keep your life on a priority system and know what must be accomplished. You can't do everything! Don't bite off more than you can chew. You can't be everything to everyone, and when you try, you risk losing sight of who you are. You become unstoppable when you work on things people can't take away from you, things like your mindset, character, and personality.

The word NO is very difficult for many of us to say yet very important to learn. To everyone who struggles to say no, it's okay to need time for yourself. Say no, not because you can't do it, or because you don't want to, but because you're a priority, too.

Don't force yourself to fit in where you don't belong. Letting toxic people go is not an act of cruelty. It's an act of self-care. I will never hate anyone, but I will distance myself from people who do not value me. That is just wise self-care.

Sometimes you have to appreciate the little things in life, like being able to see, walk, breathe, eat, and sleep. These little things are such a blessing.

Marriage is hard, divorce is hard—choose your hard! Obesity is hard, being fit is hard—choose your hard! Communication is hard, not communicating is hard—choose your hard! Being in debt is hard, being financially disciplined is hard—choose your hard! Remember, life will never be easy. It will always be hard. But we can choose our hard, so pick wisely.

Planning ahead and staying organized makes for an efficient mindset. Prepare for the unexpected things that will come your way and don't let the unexpected take over or take you down. Maintaining a positive attitude will take you much further on your life's journey than anything else.

Self-care strategies that work:

1. Disconnect on the weekend.
2. Say no – add something valuable to your life
3. Health affects the quality of life, so pay attention to your health.

4. Avoid toxic people.
5. Make alone time.
6. Spend quality time with family and friends.
7. Indulge yourself at times. It makes a huge impact.
8. Explore – watch children play, take a walk, visit a new town, etc.
9. Broaden your horizons – take a class, read a book, find what interests you.
10. Have FUN – laugh, joke, find your sense of humor!

"Life is about balance. Be kind, but don't let people abuse you. Trust, but don't be deceived. Be content, but never stop improving yourself."
~ Nishar Panwar

Elias Monitinho, Ph.D, has some strategic steps for self-care:

Step One: Take Care of Your Body

- Exercise regularly
- Eat a healthy diet
- Get 8 hours of sleep a night
- Laugh and have fun

Step Two: Take Care of Your Mind

- Develop a set of priorities
- Define your purpose in life
- Do not compare yourself to others
- Relax and do not feel guilty
- Manage technology wisely

Step Three: Take Care of Your Relationships

- Spend time with family
- Set healthy boundaries
- Learn to say "No"
- Develop a support system

Step Four: Take Care of Your Soul

- Rely on your spiritual resources
- Contemplate the heavenly reward

Respect is something one must earn. Stop focusing only on yourself and start thinking of others but don't lose balance. Don't always wait for direction from others; use your own skills and resources to solve problems. Always honor commitments and promises.

Stop using the word "sorry" over and over! People who constantly say "I'm sorry" are usually the ones not well respected. If sorry rolls off the tongue quickly and easily, one may question if it is sincere or an overused phrase.

Being a pushover is highly undesirable if your goal is to be respected. If you're too nice to everyone all of the time, some people might even think you're not genuine. Don't just take it when someone is mistreating you or taking advantage of you. Be professional and diplomatic, but don't be silent. Speaking up for yourself is not always easy to do, which is why it is the mark of a person deserving respect. You don't need to please everyone and don't be afraid of confrontation once in a while, as long as you do it in a diplomatic way.

Respect other people's time. There are so many ways we can learn this. For instance, don't be late for appointments or don't go on and on with useless chatter at meetings (and get to the point!). Respect others, even if you don't like them. And for sure, don't gossip! If you talk behind people's backs, you and your reputation will quickly become irrelevant. Every person you meet, whether you like them or not, can teach you something.

Add real value to people's lives. Think of ways to offer this value to others. When talking to others, listen and retain information from the conversations and remember things they care about the next time you see them.

You can inspire others by talking to them about your passions and goals without holding back. Offer endless encouragement to others by following their dreams, goals, and visions. Show them you have faith in them.

"Taking care of yourself is the most powerful way to begin to take care of others." ~ Bryant McGill

Taking a moment to consider a thing before you open your mouth is almost always going to command respect. Listen to others and stop talking about yourself all of the time. Start caring about others.

Respect yourself and your time. Again, by saying "no," you show you're not afraid of admitting you value your time, and you don't have time for everything. Balance. Never let success go to your head and never let failure go to your heart.

The four essential rules to being respectful:

1. **The Golden Rule** – treat others how you would like to be treated.
2. **The "It's a Small World" Rule** – you never know what might come your way in the future. Interact with everyone as a potential future employer, friend, family member, etc.
3. **The "Hidden Value" Rule** –look for the good in everyone.
4. **The "Everyone is Special" Rule** – recognize that everyone comes from a different place, and they bring vast amounts of experience and wisdom with them.

"People can let you down, but only you can keep yourself permanently down. Rise above it and get moving!" ~ Dodinsky

The Ten Commandments of Self-Care
By Valorie Burton

1. Use all of your vacation time every year.
2. Commit your time off solely to non-work-related activities.
3. Take your rest seriously.
4. Have fun at least once a week.
5. Eat regularly, preferably sitting down.
6. Exercise regularly, preferably standing up.
7. Be fruitful and productive, not busy.
8. Use technology to gain time, not consume it.
9. Connect heart-to-heart with the people who matter.
10. Be led by the Spirit.

Go TODAY and be the BEST you can be. YOU will SUCCEED!

What are some of the barriers to your self-care routine?

Why is it important to you to engage in self-care?

Show proper respect to everyone, love the family of believers, fear God, honor the emperor. (I Peter 2:17 NIV)

Finally, brethren, whatsoever things are true, whatsoever things are honest, whatsoever things are just, whatsoever things are pure, whatsoever things are lovely, whatsoever things are of good report; if there be any virtue, and if there be any praise, think on these things. (Philippians 4:8 KJV)

Let your conversation be without covetousness; and be content with such things as ye have: for he hath said, I will never leave thee, nor forsake thee. (Hebrews 13:5 KJV)

Self-Worth and Attitude

"Be proud of yourself for surviving all the silent struggles you don't speak about. In order to love who you are, you cannot hate the experiences that shaped you." ~ Sherisee

First, know your worth. Second, control your emotions. Third, never settle! ~ The Mind Journal

If your sense of self-worth is based on the approval of others, you are on a runaway roller coaster of internal conflict with no ability to control when you are up and down. Your feeling of value is at the mercy of what others think about you. Your sense of identity is determined by how others respond to you. To get off this ride and conquer your fear of rejection, allow the Lord to control your life. He created you and established your worth when He made you in His image. As you put your trust in Him, He will turn your fear into faith.

Pastor Ashley Wooldridge stated, "Control is a God category, not a human one. The more we try to control, the more chaos we create." We need to put our trust in God and let him take the wheel of our lives. If we release our control to God, things will be much easier and with a better outcome.

At a certain point, you're no longer just a product of your environment or upbringing. The way you choose to operate becomes your personal responsibility. Never accept someone's distorted view of who you are.

When you really matter to someone, that person will always make time for you. No excuses, no lies, and no broken promises. Never let a person who doesn't see your value make you forget your worth. That's their loss.

I know you are tired. I know you are physically drained. But keep believing in yourself, stay strong, and keep going. Never allow a struggle to turn your sky into a ceiling. You must believe there's always a way. Don't focus on who has let you down. Appreciate who has lifted you up. Enjoy every moment you have. Because in life, there are no rewinds and life is short...

Don't worry. They'll realize your worth when they can't find someone like you.

Suffering In Silence

"Attitude is a little thing that makes a big difference!"
~ Winston Churchill

A positive attitude can change your life. If you look at the bright side of life, your whole life becomes filled with light. Think positively! A BAD attitude is like a flat tire—it can't get you far unless you change it!

We are all very guilty of taking too many things in life for granted. Learn to express gratitude for all of the things you take for granted. Believe in yourself and your abilities. All success begins with believing in ourselves. Focus on keeping a positive attitude and look for the good in every situation!

"Your attitude, not your aptitude, will determine your altitude."
~ Zig Ziglar

Steps to improve your attitude:

- Our attitude is our choice—only we can change it. Take charge of your attitude as it will affect your future and your health.
- Make your diet a well-balanced diet. Limit your fats, sugars, and sodium.
- Be sure to include a minimum of 30 minutes a day of exercise. This will help you stay active, better your circulation, and it's great for the mind.
- Healthy relationships not only help control your stress levels but also keep you socially active. This is very important to help ward off depression and loneliness.
- Without goals, how do you measure success? Without successes, how do you stay motivated?

"The longer I live, the more I realize the impact of attitude on life. Attitude, to me, is more important than facts. It is more important than the past, than education, than money, than circumstances, than failures, than successes, than what other people think or say or do. It is more important than appearance and giftedness. It will make or break an organization, a church...a home. The remarkable thing is we have a choice every day regarding the attitude we will embrace for that day. We cannot change our past. We cannot change the fact that people will act in a certain way. We cannot change the inevitable. The only thing we can do is play on the one string we have, and that is our attitude. I am convinced that life is 10 percent what happens to me and 90 percent how I react to it. And so it is with you...we are in change of our Attitudes." ~ Charles Swindoll

How to Form a Positive Attitude:

- **Give thanks for each day** – express gratitude for all the things you take for granted.
- **Count your personal blessings** – things like a clear mind, fit body, leisure time, etc.
- **Do a good deed without telling anyone** – there are plenty of good deeds waiting to be done.
- **Forgive an old hurt** – you will feel freer, stronger, and overall, better.
- **Ask to be forgiven** – if you have wronged someone, it is time to ask forgiveness.
- **Appreciate your belongings** – be thankful for everything, large or small, that you have.

- **Compliment someone** – you will feel good improving someone's day.
- **Admire the view** – go outside, find a comfortable place to sit, and enjoy the scenery around you.
- **Donate something** – give something to someone who can use it. People in need do appreciate receiving something they are in need of.
- **Volunteer to help the needy** – you will feel needed and appreciated.
- **Sing a song** – it's hard to stay in a bad mood when you sing!
- **Smile** – a smile is contagious and promotes good will as well as a favorable impression.
- **Expect success and not failure** – think on the positive versus the negative.
- **Believe in yourself and your abilities** – all success begins with believing in ourselves.

Health benefits of positive thinking:

- Increased life span
- Lower rates of depression
- Lower levels of distress
- Greater resistance to the common cold
- Better psychological and physical well-being
- Reduced risk of death from cardiovascular disease
- Better coping skills during hardships and times of stress

Here are some great quotes to post on your mirror and recite everyday as you get ready for your day:

"Life has no remote, get up and change it yourself." ~ Mark A Cooper

"Weakness of attitude becomes weakness of character."
~ Albert Einstein

"Our favorite attitude should be gratitude." ~ Zig Ziglar

The goal of positive thinking is to give yourself a more positive attitude about yourself, all the while seeing yourself honestly and accepting yourself. It helps to remove the internal barriers that can keep you from doing your best.

Try to avoid extreme thinking word choices such as " I always" or "I'll never!" The next time you start giving yourself a browbeating, tell yourself to stop it. We all have flaws and make mistakes. Perfection is a high goal to aim for and none ever get there! Replace your criticism with encouragement. You are not to blame every time something goes wrong or someone has a problem. This was a very tough lesson for me to learn because our dad blamed us kids for everything!

Just as everything is not your fault, not everything is your responsibility. It's okay to be helpful, but don't feel the need to be all things and do all things for all people. Just as you can't make other people happy, don't expect others to make you feel happy or good about yourself. You create your own feelings and make your own decisions. Keep your statements positive, not negative, and focus on what you're able to do.

Suffering In Silence

"Do not let your happiness depend on something you may love."
~ C.S. Lewis

Sometimes people pretend that you're a bad person so they don't feel guilty about the things they did to you. Don't worry about what people say behind your back. They are the people who find faults in your life (or someone else's) instead of fixing the faults in their own life. You can't force people to respect you, but you can refuse to tolerate their disrespect. The best feeling is when you realize your self-worth and then handle a situation far better than what your old self would have done.

"Worry about your character, not your reputation. Your character is who you are. Your reputation is who people think you are."
~ John Wooden

The reality is you have to work at healing yourself without becoming like those who traumatize you. There is nothing more heartbreaking than witnessing a woman question her self-worth after being badly treated by a man. Self-worth was something our mom struggled with. As soon as she gained a little self-worth and self-esteem, it would be taken from her.

The hardest lesson is realizing you can't make someone value you. You can show up, give your best, and love deeply – but if they don't see it, that's on them, not you. Your worth doesn't disappear just because they fail to notice. Never feel guilty for moving on from anyone who, though they had the chance to treat you better, never thought you were worth it.

Suffering In Silence

"I can do all things through Christ who strengthens me!"
(Philippians 4:13 NKJV)

Being around the wrong environment and wrong people will make you forget your worth. Stay focused. The red flags you once ignored become deal breakers when you know your worth. Don't let yourself be controlled by three things: people, money, or past experiences. Instead be controlled by Positive Things!

Not every day is a good day—live anyway.

Not everyone will tell you the truth—be honest anyway.

Not all you love will love you back—love anyway.

Live by 3 simple rules:

- Love needs action
- Trust needs proof
- Sorry needs change

You're a fighter. Look at everything you've overcome. Don't give up now.

How is your attitude?

Are you living your life to its fullest?

Do everything without grumbling or arguing, so that you may become blameless and pure, "children of God without fault in a warped and crooked generation." Then you will shine among them like stars in the sky. (Philippians 2:14-15 NIV)

Suffering In Silence

For the word of God is alive and active. Sharper than any double-edged sword, it penetrates even to dividing soul and spirit, joints and marrow; it judges the thoughts and attitudes of the heart.
(Hebrews 4:12 NIV)

11
What's Your Story

"Your dreams count, your voice matters, your story is important and needs to be heard, your life has a purpose; you were born to make an IMPACT!" ~ Unknown Author

You can't go back and change the beginning, but you can start where you are and change the ending. So never give up and focus on the road ahead of you!

Everyone has their own story. Everyone knows their own pain. Never allow anyone to judge your path. Because only you know how much strength it took to get up and continue to GO ON! Never forget how brave it is to continue to show up in a story that looks so different that what you thought it would be.

Past

Don't allow your past to determine your future! ~ Author Unkonwn

"If you don't leave your past in the past, it will destroy your future. Live for what today has to offer, not what yesterday has taken away." ~ Mother Teresa

**The past is your lesson. The present is your gift.
The future is your motivation!**

We all have standards, habits, and comfort zones into which we retreat, even when we're given opportunities to improve ourselves. This results in keeping us exactly where we are, even though we believe we want to improve our situation.

"Information is not knowledge. The only source of knowledge is experience. You need experience to gain wisdom." ~ Albert Einstein

"The 3 Cs in life: Choice, Chance, and Change. You must make the choice to take the chance if you want anything in life to change."
~ Zig Ziglar

"One day at a time is all we should be dealing with. We can't go back to yesterday and we can't control tomorrow, so live for today."
~ Author Unknown

If you continue to carry the bricks from your past, you will end up building the same house. If you don't leave your past in the past, it will destroy your future. Live for what today has to offer, not what yesterday has taken away. The truth is we all have a sad story to some extent. Either make it your excuse or make it your motivation. That's entirely up to you! However, be kind to the past versions of yourself that didn't know the things you now know.

Life doesn't allow us to go back and fix what we have done wrong in the past, but it does allow us to live each day better than our last. We all have a past. We all made choices that might not have been the best ones. None of us are completely innocent, but we all get a fresh start every day to be a better person than we were before.

Don't waste time thinking about what you could have done differently. Keep your eyes on the road ahead and do it differently now. Don't give up because of one bad chapter in your life but learn from it. Keep going. Your story does not end here. You don't have to understand the entire path to take the first step. Sometimes your next chapter begins with courage, not clarity, and faith is what carries you through the unknown. ***Your past can control you if you don't control it***.

Some people not only get stuck in the past but begin to believe they don't deserve anything better! They have become so beaten down that they begin to believe those who have attacked them verbally.

Are you stuck in the past?

No matter what has happened in the past, God will meet you where you are today and take you where you need to be tomorrow. Accept your past without regret, handle your past with confidence, and face your future without fear.

Stop staring at the closed door!

4 ways to overcome unexpected change
By Valorie Burton

1. **Mourn the loss.**
   It can feel devastating when unwelcome change intrudes on your life. Give yourself permission to grieve your loss. Acknowledge any lessons you've learned. Once you've acknowledged and mourned, choose to pick yourself

up, dust yourself off, and move forward. Self-pity is self-sabotage.

2. **Make a decision to face forward.**

   At some point, you must stop lingering at the closed door as though it will reopen. Instead, walk away and take steps onto the path that is unfolding before you. Face forward rather than backwards, and you'll find that change offers new hope and opportunity. This decision takes courage. Courage is a choice.

3. **Be open to change.**

   Don't compare your new opportunities to your old opportunities. Instead, recognize that new opportunities sometimes have very different benefits from old ones. They sometimes address different needs and wants, and bring you joy in ways that were missing before. Sometimes they stretch you in ways you haven't been stretched. Embrace the challenge with gratitude and perseverance.

4. **Walk through the open doors.**

   New life, new work, and new opportunities will open up on your path. Walk through them!

Often, doors close because we never should have walked through them in the first place. At other times, they close because they were meant only for a season. Learn the lessons, live with courage, and enjoy the journey.

"Forget the former things; do not dwell on the past. See, I am doing a new thing! Now it springs up; do you not perceive it? I am making a way in the wilderness and streams in the wasteland."
(Isaiah 43:18-19 NIV)

*Jesus says, "No one who puts a hand to the plow and looks back is fit
for service in the kingdom of God." (Luke 9:62 NIV)*

Present

*"This chapter of my life is called: Now that I know better,
I must do better." ~* Maya Angelou

*"You can't change the past and can't predict the future, but you can
ruin the present by worrying about both." ~* Author Unknown

*"Accept your past without regret, handle your present with
confidence, and face your future without fear."*
~ Nicholas Sansbury Smith

*Each new chapter of our lives requests an old part of us to fall
and a new part of us to rise. ~* Jenna Galbut

We are God's warriors; I have survived mental abuse, sexual abuse, and a car crash off a bridge into a lake! Whatever your hurdle in life may be, you can get past it.

I believe in YOU!

Remember that life exists outside of your head. Sometimes we get too tangled in our thoughts and forget to live in the present. Don't give up because of one bad chapter in your life. Keep going. Your story doesn't end here!

People wait all day for 5 p.m. All week for Friday. All summer for winter. All winter for summer. All of life for happiness. Don't let the pursuit of tomorrow diminish the joy of today. Enjoy the moment—enjoy today.

"Make NOW the best it can be; make NOW your priority.
What you think and do NOW determines your future."
~ Marilyn and Larry Singer

There are two things we get every day—a chance and a choice. Don't wait for your ship to come in...swim out to it. Try something new, something above and beyond what you have already mastered, and you will grow.

Key aspects of living in the present:

- Mindfulness – pay attention to your thoughts
- Awareness of surroundings – notice what is happening around you and engage
- Acceptance of the present – tolerating both pleasant and unpleasant experiences
- Focus on one task at a time – avoid multitasking when possible
- Practice gratitude – appreciate the small moments in life

Benefits of living in the present:

- Reduces stress and anxiety
- Improves focus and concentration
- Greater appreciation for life
- Enhanced relationships
- Increased self-awareness

Are you allowing your past to determine your future?

What is the purpose of your past and how can you use it to help others?

"Therefore do not be anxious about tomorrow, for tomorrow will be anxious for itself. Sufficient for the day is its own trouble.
(Matthew 6:34 ESV)

"This is the day that the LORD has made; let us rejoice and be glad in it." (Psalm 118:24 ESV)

Future

"Don't be afraid to start over again. This time you're not starting from scratch, you're starting from experience." ~ Author Unknown

"The best way to predict the future is to dream it." ~ Alan Kay

One day you will tell your story of how you overcame what you went through. It will be someone else's survival guide. Today, find your reason and find your purpose! Do not waste time thinking about what you could have done differently. Keep your eyes on the road ahead and do it differently now. You don't have to understand the entire path to take the first step. Sometimes, your next chapter begins with courage, not clarity.

And faith is what carries you through the unknown.

You must make a decision that you are going to move on. It won't happen automatically. You will have to rise up and say, "I don't care how hard this is, I don't care how disappointed I am, I'm not going to let this get the best of me. I'm moving on with my life. Unless you can visualize it, you won't ever be able to actually accomplish it.

"The best revenge is moving on with your life. Not anger. Not proving a point. Not getting even. Just peace. Let them watch you heal. Let them see you unbothered. Nothing shakes someone who tried to break you more than watching you live free, whole, and completely out of reach." ~ Robert Wilkinson

Find comfort in knowing that even if it's not today, one day you will truly understand why things turned out the way they did. Discipline is explaining to your brain that you need to sacrifice immediate pleasures for greater rewards in the future. The life in front of you is far more important than the life behind you.

"We are all just a car crash, a diagnosis, an unexpected phone call, a newfound love, or a broken heart away from becoming a completely different person. How beautifully fragile are we that so many things can take but a moment to alter who we are for forever?"
~ Samuel Decker Thompson

Remove yourself from any situation that feels like a repeat of your past. Instead of thinking how hard the journey is, think of how great your story will be! Everyone has a story, and someone needs to hear it. Reset... restart... refocus... as many times as you need to.

JUST don't quit.

"In their hearts humans plan their course, but the Lord establishes their steps. (Proverbs 16:9 NIV)

Don't get in the way of opportunities just because you can't always see a specific and definitive path to the results you want. You don't need to see the path—you just need to have and hold the vision of what you want. The clearer the vision, the better chance of achieving it. Think about that for a moment. If you don't have a clear picture of your desire, how in the world will you know when it shows up?

Ways to stay out of your own way:

- Think creatively
- Increase your awareness of everything around you
- Associate with successful people
- Raise the level of your circle of friends and associates
- Take advantage of opportunities
- Follow your instincts

Taking chances is part of life. If you're not willing to take risks, you won't get any rewards in return. (However, you can't chase every rabbit that passes through your yard!) Each opportunity knocks only once. If you don't answer the door, someone else will. The worst days of your life and the best days of your life can just be a day apart, so keep moving forward! In life, setbacks aren't the end; they're set-ups for your next victory. Stay focused. Keep pushing forward.

What does your ideal future look like?

**What are the first steps you can take
towards your ideal future?**

**Keep Trying!
Keep Reaching!
Keep Dreaming!**

"Keep your dreams alive." ~ Gail Devers

"Everything starts with a dream." ~ Author Unknown

Nothing beautiful ever came from an easy life. Nothing truly incredible ever came from times of ease and contentment. We naturally want to reach for more. Allow yourself to embrace the journey of life but rest at whatever step you're at and enjoy it as you'll never be back there again. Just rest though—don't get stuck there! Nothing remains for too long, not even our sorrows.

The only thing that is withholding you from your own happiness is YOU. If you want to change, then change. Acting on it is crucial. Nowhere were you ever told or taught that you would live in a magnificent land of beauty and happiness every day, remember that.

It is always better to be someone who tried and failed as opposed to someone who was too weak to even try. If you're genuinely unhappy, there's only one thing you must do to change everything: think differently! The first steps are always the hardest—take the first step and begin your journey of life. Your story is not finished yet. You'll soon laugh in the places you have cried. Keep going. God is with you.

Also, don't get caught up drowning in information while starving for wisdom. Just keep moving forward. Don't waste time thinking about what you could have done differently. Keep your eyes on the road ahead and do it differently now.

You're not defined by the storms you face but by the light you carry through them. Your kindness, resilience, and hope make you unbreakable, and even when the winds howl, your spirit whispers, "I will not be moved; I will rise stronger than ever."

"Don't forget, that even when life gets hard and you feel like giving up, there is a future that you haven't seen yet. Stay strong, believe in yourself, and never stop moving forward." ~ Roger Lee

"Without God, life has no purpose, and without purpose, life has no meaning. Without meaning, life has no significance or hope."
~ Rick Warren

What are your biggest dreams?

What are the biggest challenges or fears you have about pursuing your dreams?

"For I know the plans I have for you," declares the LORD, "plans to prosper you and not to harm you, plans to give you a hope and a future." (Jeremiah 29:11 NIV)

Many are the plans in a person's heart, but it is the Lord's purpose that prevails. (Proverbs 19:21 NIV)

We can make our plans, but the LORD determines our steps.
(Proverbs 16:9 NLT)

Life Is Like a Rose

By Joanne R Kanute

We all come from different types of soil and growing seasons—some rich, some rocky, others sandy. Our growing conditions and seasons are all different. We all gain our nourishment in different ways, yet each and every one of us is beautiful in our own way.

The complexity of a rose is much like the complexity of our lives. A thorny stem provides protection to us as we grow yet it also represents the unpleasant issues we go through in life. As we grow and mature, we become stronger and more resilient as we bloom.

Each delicate petal forms and each gives off a sweet smell. Each rose forms a soft silky beautiful shape of its own in its own vibrant color. Much like each one of us, we all come from different backgrounds and come through many different struggles in life. We all survive on various nourishments yet when we come together as a group, we form a beautiful bouquet!

10 Questions To Focus On The Rest Of Your Life

1. What is my single greatest strength?
2. What three decisions are causing me the greatest stress?
3. What is overwhelming me?
4. What impossible roadblock has me stuck?
5. If I could only do three things in my lifetime, what would they be?
6. What should I resign from or drop out of?

7.   What can I postpone?
8.   What things on my to-do list can someone else do 80 percent as well?
9.   What are the elephants on my schedule?
10. What are the three things I could do in the next 90 days to make a 50 percent difference in reaching short term goals and resolving immediate problems?

Benefits of Working with a Coach

Take more, better and smarter actions...
because you set the goals that you really want

Have a balanced life that works well...
because you designed it for yourself

Make and keep more money...
You are worth more than you are making

Reach for more – much more...
And not be consumed in the process

Make better decisions for yourself and your business...
Because your focus is clear

Have a lot more sustainable energy...
No more chugging along

What to talk about with your coach

How are you?

- How are you feeling about yourself – the good and the bad
- How you look at your life
- How you feel about others

What has happened since the last call?

- What has happened to you since the last call?
- Shifts, wins, and insights
- New choices or decisions made
- Personal news

What are you working on?

- Progress report on your goals, projects, and activities
- What you've done that you are proud of
- What you are coming up against

How can I help?

- Where are you stuck?
- Is there something that you're wondering about?
- A plan of action

What is next?

- What is the next goal or project to take on?
- What is the next goal or distinction to understand?
- What do you want next for yourself?

Bibliography

Boundaries by June Hunt

Self-worth by June Hunt

Say No by Dr. Townsend and Dr. Cloud

Manipulation – Cutting the Strings of Control by June Hunt

How to Deal With Rageaholic by Malaysha Castillo

Rageaholic: Definition, Signs and Treatments by Renee Skedel, LPC

Clear Your Clutter, Clear Your Mind by Valorie Burton

Rejection: Healing a Wounded Heart by June Hunt

Verbal and Emotional Abuse: Victory Over Verbal and Emotional Abuse by June Hunt

Stress: How to Cope at the End of Your Rope by June Hunt

Financial Freedom: How to Manage Your Money Wisely by June Hunt

Putting Anger to Work for You by Ruth and Joel Schroeder

Assert Yourself by Lisa Contini

Get Out of Your Way by Marilyn and Larry Singer

Confronting Without Offending by Deborah Smith Pegues

Healing for Damaged Emotions by David A Seamands

Boundaries by Dr. Townsend and Dr. Cloud

Author Biography
Of Joanne R. Kanute

Joanne R. Kanute became a licensed cosmetologist in 1982. Not long in the industry, she realized hair was a small part of what happened in the chair! Many clients sought guidance to many of their problems, and they felt safe to discuss that with their hairstylist. She became a Board Certified Master Certified Life Coach and pursued her bachelor's in counseling. Joanne refers to herself as a Life Coach Hair Stylist.

Joanne is a firm believer in lifelong learning! As you can see, from her additional education listed in the back of the book, she practices what she preaches.

- Board Certified Master Certified Life Coach
- Certified Master Image Consultant
- Bachelors of Christian Counseling
- Licensed Cosmetologist

Joanne is the CEO of Unlimited Creations. She is a life coach, speaker, author, cosmetologist, and owner of four successful businesses. She works with women on strengthening their self-esteem with "God's truth about YOU!" She has over 40 years of experience building women's self-esteem as she walks beside them, encouraging them to keep moving forward in life. Joanne was featured on the front cover of the National Association of Christian Women Entrepreneur's magazine in 2015.

As a life coach, she challenges woman to not only continue moving forward in their journey of life but helps strengthen their self-esteem and increase their internal/external self- image. She believes that if we are looking for different results, we must be willing to make some changes in our lives. She believes in setting your eyes on your goals with your feet moving forward, staying focused, and being ready for change!

Joanne is the author of *Who Told You The Lie? Strengthen Your Self-esteem with God's Truth About You.* Her book is published in English and Spanish. She has also published a number of blog articles covering various subject matters pertaining to life in today's world and encouraging her readers to continually move forward.

Joanne survived an automobile accident in 1976. The steering went out of the car she was driving, and she and her passengers went off a bridge into a lake. The miracle is that everyone survived with only minor injuries. It just so happened the bridge she went off was located on a country gravel road and the accident is how she met her husband. It was by the entrance to the driveway of her future husband's family farm! However, it wasn't love at first sight! Her future husband came down to the bridge with his Polaroid camera taking pictures, saying

"No one has ever gone off this bridge before." As he walked away, headed back up their driveway, he muttered "women drivers" as he shook his head. We have now been married for 48 years!

When she awakens every morning, her goal is to make a positive impact on someone's life. When she is not coaching, creating behind the salon chair, writing, or speaking, you can find her reading, traveling, engaged in diamond art projects, or spending time with her family and playing with her grandchildren.

> **Her motto is:** Be the BEST you can be! Keep traveling forward on the journey of life.
> **Her mission:** Yesterday is gone and we can't dwell on it or change the past. Tomorrow may never come so don't become consumed or worry about tomorrow. Learn to enjoy today before it becomes yesterday!
> **Her purpose:** Life is about choices. As your coach, she will help you navigate through your journey of life and show you how to make good choices.
> **Her Goal:** To not only make you look great, but make you feel great about yourself! Her business is about YOU!

What one thing in your life do you want to change the most?

Author website and Social Media:

Website: www.unlimitedcreations.net
Email: jk.unlimitedcreations@gmail.com
Follow me on: Facebook, Instagram, LinkedIn and X

Endorsements:

Joanne is an intelligent, capable, dedicated, and personable woman. She is always quick on her feet with sensible reactions in all circumstances. She possesses and demonstrates outstanding leadership abilities, unsurpassed organizational skills, and an exceptional desire to provide the best services she can for people in any capacity. ~ Cindie S. Tucson, AZ

Joanne, I need your pep talks every day. ~ Rhonda J. Tucson, AZ

Joanne is sensitive to individual confidences and can be expected to maintain any client relationship with strict confidentiality. ~ Roland D. Tucson, AZ

There are just some things you don't want to discuss with your family or friends. I always look forward to being able to come see Joanne and bounce off problems or ideas with her. I know it doesn't go anywhere else. ~ Rachel Garrett Surprise, AZ

I always feel better after I have had the opportunity to talk with Joanne. ~ Karen Tessitore Surprise, AZ

Associations

AACC – The American Association of Christian Counselors
BCLC – Board of Christian Life Coach
IBCC – International Board of Christian Care
PBA – Professional Beauty Association

Author's Education:

BCMCLC	Life Coach	Light University
Bachelor's	Christian Counseling	International Institute of Christian Counseling
Graduate	Licensed Cosmetology	Ritter School of Beauty
Graduate	Professional Fitness & Nutrition	Professional Career Development Institute
Under Grad	Dale Carnegie	University of Central Missouri
Certificate	Introduction to Business	Pima Community College
Certificate	Professional Interior Design	Sheffield School of Interior Design
Certificate	Fashion Merchandising	Penn Foster Career School
Certificate	Health & Wellness Coaching	Light University
Certificate	Leadership Coaching	Light University
Certificate	Stress & Trauma	Light University
Certificate	Extraordinary Women	Light University
Certificate	Marriage Works	Light University
Certificate	Financial Coaching	Light University
Certificate	Advanced Life Coaching	Light University
Certificate	Professional Life Coaching 101	Light University
Certificate	Professional Life Coaching 201	Light University
Certificate	Executive & Organizational Coaching	Light University
Certificate	Breaking Free	Light University
Certificate	Relationship Coaching	Light University
Certificate	Women's Coaching	Light University
Certificate	Gerontology and Aging 101	Light University
Certificate	Gerontology and Aging 201	Light University
Certificate	Christian Counseling Skills & Techniques	Light University
Certificate	Christian Counseling 2.0	Light University
Certificate	Soul Care & Biblically Counseling 2.0	Light University

Certificate	Hope Counseling	Light University
Certificate	Life Recovery Coaching 101	Light University
Certificate	Counseling Women Master Toolkit	Light University
Certificate	Peace Making & Conflict Resolution 2.0	Light University
Certificate	Perfectionism 2.0	Light University
Certificate	Coffee Cup Counselling	Light University
Certificate	Dr. Trent Relationship Coaching	Light University
Certificate	Narcissism 2.0	Light University
Certificate	Alcoholism 2.0	Light University
Certificate	Weight Management Challenge 2.0	Light University
Certificate	Caring For People God's Way	Light University
Certificate	Stop Procrastinating	Fred Pryor
Certificate	Staying Positive	Fred Pryor
Certificate	Six Wrong Ways To Manage	Fred Pryor
Certificate	SMART Goals	Fred Pryor
Certificate	Motivational Leadership	Fred Pryor
Certificate	Developing Yourself	Fred Pryor
Certificate	Dealing With Resistance	Fred Pryor
Certificate	Leadership Daily Checklist	Fred Pryor
Certificate	Leadership Styles	Fred Pryor
Certificate	The Coaching Process	Fred Pryor
Certificate	Introduction to Coaching	Fred Pryor
Certificate	Adapting Your Style	Fred Pryor
Certificate	Building an Effective Leadership Team	Fred Pryor
Certificate	Assertiveness Without Aggressiveness	Fred Pryor
Certificate	Clinical Depression and the Restless Mind	AACC
Certificate	Celebrate Faith	AACC
Certificate	Coaching Skills Introduction	Fred Pryor
Certificate	Assertive Communication Skills for Women	Fred Pryor

Certificate	Business Writing & Grammar Essentials	New Horizons Learning Center
Certificate	Certified Image Consultant	TEB Associates International
Certificate	Certified Master Image Consultant	TEB Associates International
Certificate	Nutritional Consultant	Global College of Natural Medicine
Certificate	Professional Fitness & Nutrition Program	The School of Fitness and Nutrition
Certificate	Color Consultant Technician	Color Me Beautiful Costa Mesa, CA
Certificate	Grief and Mental Health in Youth	AACC
Certificate	Challenges, Pitfalls and Concerns	AACC
Certificate	The Power of Positivity & Motivation	AACC
Certificate	Addiction and Recovery	AACC
Certificate	Grief and Mental Health in Youth II	AACC
Certificate	Childhood Grief, Loss & Trauma	AACC
Certificate	Faith & Disciplines in Therapy	AACC
Certificate	Religious Liberty	AACC
Certificate	Trauma, Mental Health Part 2	AACC
Certificate	Social Isolation, Loneliness and Meaningful Relationships	AACC
Certificate	Money, Finances and Relationships	AACC
Certificate	Research, Best Practices and Mental Healthcare	AACC
Certificate	Marital Conflict, Separation and Divorce	AACC
Certificate	Sleep, Diet, Wellness & Performance	AACC
Certificate	Attachments	Light University
Certificate	Leading Small Groups: The Basics	Light University
Certificate	Certified Senior Advisor	Society of Certified Senior Advisors
Certificate	Body Contouring 6 in 1 Masterclass	Body Contouring Academy
Certificate	Certified Group Facilitator	Christian Women's Leadership Institute
Certificate	Developing Emotional Intelligence	Fred Pryor
Certificate	Living Well	Stanford University

9 781945 464317